Footsteps of the Mountain Spirits...

APPALACHIA

Myths, Legends, and Landscapes of the Southern Highlands

Late summer on Little Hump Mountain

Kenneth Murray

The Overmountain Press

JOHNSON CITY, TENNESSEE

— OTHER BOOKS BY KENNETH MURRAY —

DOWN TO EARTH — PEOPLE OF APPALACHIA
A PORTRAIT OF APPALACHIA
HIGHLAND TRAILS: A Guide to Scenic Walking and Riding Trails (Revised 1992)

A nationally-acclaimed photographer, Kenneth Murray's work has been widely exhibited and published. His photographs have appeared in *Time, New York Times, People, Wilderness,* and publications of the Appalachian Trail Conference, as well as other magazines and newspapers. A native of the Appalachian region, Murray's love of the highlands led to his quest to find and photograph the essence of the region's natural beauty. His trail guide grew from a desire to share not only those photographs but the joy of that experience. He has previously produced two highly acclaimed photographic essays; and the collection found within this volume will be a treasured keepsake.

A thing of beauty is a joy for ever....
John Keats,
Endymion, 1818

Climb the mountains and get their good tidings. Nature's peace will flow into you as sunshine flows into trees. The winds will blow their own freshness into you, and the storms their energy, while cares will drop off like autumn leaves.

—John Muir, 1911

Young dogwoods and mountain maples form the under story beneath sugar maples and other hardwoods on Mount Mitchell in the North Carolina Black Mountains.

How the Appalachian Mountains Came to Be

Once in a faraway time, when all was water, the Grandmother earth lay beneath the seas. All the animals and people lived in the world above the sky's arch, but because it was very crowded, they were anxious to find a new home. They knew that there was land beneath the waters, but numerous attempts to bring it to the surface, even with the help of all the gathered creatures, had failed. But one day the little Water Beetle dove to the bottom and brought up some soft mud. Somehow the tiny speck of earth began to grow and spread on every side. It grew and grew, until it became the great floating island which is the land.

In the beginning the earth was soft and without form, so a great Bird was sent out to find dry ground and make it ready for them. He flew for a long time over all the damp land until He became very tired. Becoming weaker and weaker, He could barely fly at all. Struggling to stay airborne, His wings began to strike the wet earth, and where they struck the ground there was a valley created, and wherever they turned up again a mountain arose.

When those watching from above saw this they were afraid that the whole world would be turned into mountains and called Him back. But the Appalachian country remains full of mountains to this day.

—Retold from James Mooney's
Myths of the Cherokee

Drawn from the genesis myths of the Cherokee, this and numerous other stories give superior powers to great ancestral spirits, animals, monsters, giants and little people. Much of the lore had religious significance, passed on family, clan and tribal histories, or illustrated morals of right conduct. Other stories explained a mysterious world. Even yarns intended merely to entertain personalized relationships to the elements, kinship with all living things, and man's dependency on the natural world. Each tribe's body of knowledge passed through an intricate web of myths, legends and religious formulas, the telling of which required great narrative skills and practiced memory.

Modern geologists piece together other stories to explain the rise of the Appalachian Mountains, incredible as any of the ancient myths, involving incomprehensible spans of time and cataclysmic events. One theory tells of another great continent which once stood here. It was eroded and carried away a grain at a time to form a vast plain and shallow sea; then earthquakes, volcanoes and slipping continental masses erected the Blue Ridge chain of mountains where they now stand. This drama unfolded before there was life on the planet, more than 500 million years ago. The parallel Cumberland/Allegheny range, with its sedimentary layers of coal, limestone, and sandstone, arose much later.

By the time the first Europeans visited the Appalachian mountains, the region had seen the passing of several migrating groups. The nations living in the mountain shadows combined agriculture, domesticated animals and hunting for their livelihoods. Sophisticated theologies had also evolved, possibly including a dominant "Great Spirit", although not necessarily monotheism since much of their ancient lore was interwoven. Exploits of the "Ancients" were passed through generations by storytellers beside fires that danced and cast ominous, spooky shadows on the screen of looming forest at the edge of evening camps. Early travelers among the Indians, such as James Adair who lived among the Cherokees, Creeks and Chickasaws, compared their elaborate systems of law and structured societies with those of the olden tribes of Israel.

The Southern Appalachian region was dominated by the Cherokees, but they were probably pushed into the region through generations of war with the Iroquois federation, especially the Senecas. Their migration narratives and early historical accounts place them much farther north, in Ohio, Virginia and West Virginia. They either displaced or absorbed earlier groups that had made their homes in the foothills. Intertribal warfare continued into the pioneer settlement era.

At the arrival of European traders and immigrants, much of the region between the parallel Blue Ridge and Cumberland ranges was a vast no-man's-land. Perhaps it was used as a common hunting preserve by surrounding tribes, or through mutual agreement, it served as a buffer between hostile groups. The competing groups included the Tuscarora and Catawba to the east, Creeks, Chickasaw, Shawnee and Yuchi to the south and west, and Seneca, Delaware and others to the north.

The story of how the mountains came to be peopled is only partly revealed by archaeologists, oral tradition, and written records. Where the first inhabitants of the region came from, or where they went, is lost in the eternal wanderings of the early human tribe; even their names are beyond the pale of memory. But one image seems clear throughout its early tenancy—it was a bountiful land of plenty, a limitless larder of the fruits of fecund soils, forest and animals—a new Eden, a paradise on earth, a land where disease and want were rare. Indian nations of the mountain foothills were remarkably hardy due to factors such as rigorous lifestyle, clean air and water, varied and healthful diet, low population densities, sterilizing effects of passing through the cold of arctic regions during long migrations, and the frequent moving of villages as soils became less productive or game overhunted. They had few maladies; even the common cold and baldness were rare.

The American Indians are frequently discussed as if they were a homogenous group, but there were substantial differences between the tribes. They ranged in stature from six or seven feet tall, near giants by European standards of the discovery era when the average male stood well under five feet tall, to near pygmies. Coloring of the "red man" varied from near white to near black. The numerous languages spoken were incomprehensible to each other. In the eastern Woodlands there were more than 125 distinct tribal groups. Although never numbering more than 25,000, loosely grouped in the southern mountains, the Cherokees were probably the largest of these aboriginal nations. In this varied patchwork a common thread of trade and sign language developed, woodland paths linked scattered bands, and many myths and ideas were shared.

Much of life was out-of-doors, on intimate terms with the land, forest, fellow creatures and forces of weather. All animate things were thought to contain the sacred spark of life, even the stones which sometimes moved, and their spirits were revered with humility and oneness. Existence for those who walked the surface of the earth was an uncertain, delicate balance, subject to the fickle whims of nature's forces and the interwoven spirits of all life. Hunting and warfare were accompanied with great ritual and atonement to the spirits of those slain. Unnecessary killing was avoided, even of wolves and rattlesnakes. But all was not idyllic. While it was a land of plenty, it also was isolated and sometimes a harsh realm dominated by survival of only the fit. Superstition and taboos held sway. Cruelties of constant testing and warfare were the norm among neighboring bands. Setting fires to drive game, uncovering chestnuts for harvest, clearing crop lands, or improving berry grounds was practiced, and sometimes forests were destroyed in the process.

It was a howling, immense wilderness, and people were an insignificant part of the vastness. Through generations in the shadow of almighty hills and towering forests, myths grew to envelop all natural forces and the great swinging moods of the seasons. Every landmark was intimately woven into the fabric of life along the sylvan ridges and

and etched away. But the forests are resilient and the noble highlands still offer their blessings and uplift spirits that trod their ancient pathways—paths once worn deep by herds of bison, elk, and deer and by moccasin-clad feet of hunters that pursued them, long forgotten, distant eons before the first jumbo jet or all-terrain vehicle.

The less tangible aesthetics of sights, sounds and spiritual oneness with the natural world recedes before the rise of materialism and fast-paced demands for instant gratification in our spectator societies. In the struggle between those who would preserve the small remaining heritage of wild and natural places and others seeking to subdivide and develop every acre at a profit, the latter group seems to have the upper hand. And the gods seem far away.

How in this struggle can the value of stepping back into the quiet pace of our ancestors counter the hunger for quick profits? Speculation in Appalachian soil has long been an honored, even revered, profession. A list of those who have been involved in land schemes in the mountains reads like a ''Who's Who'' of national and regional heroes. In the Blue Ridge the assault on the remaining sanctuary of wild places is led by second home, resort and tourist trap developers, while the Cumberlands are being sacrificed to wildcat strip mine operators and gas and oil drilling to supply cheap energy. Is even a small corner of wilderness to remain? Perhaps we can relearn the ancient wisdom that the earth is more than a commodity.

When the first nomadic hunter gatherers wandered into the southern mountains of Appalachia at least twelve thousand years ago, the highlands were already ancient. So ancient that they defy human concept of time; time so vast that all the generations of the family of man would be only a heartbeat to the gentle giants. But time has taken its revenge on once lofty peaks that stood near the creation, reducing them to mere shadows of their former spires. Springing from the void, when even the Earth Mother was young, possibly reaching a height of 35,000 feet, they watched as lesser worlds rose and sank beneath the seas. The Appalachians were among the Earth's eldest children,

Catawba rhododendron blooms in field of blackberry blossoms on Grassy Ridge Bald along the Tennessee/North Carolina border.

river plains with legends of monsters and nymphs, giants, supermen and little people. It was a revered and sacred world with shadows of ancestral spirits watching from the enchanted highlands.

Early European visitors passing through lofty gaps were awed by the vast, blue-green sea of mountains spreading like a great ocean to infinity. Passing beneath the regal canopy of trees was compared to walking through an endless, vaulted cathedral.

Much of that grandeur has been squandered, dissected

Catawba rhododendron catch the colors of the sunset and evening sky along the Roan Highlands near the junction of the Appalachian and Grassy Ridge Bald Trails.

grew to be her tallest, and in beauty none were ever more favored. A dark, solemn forest towered overhead, reducing to insignificance the passing of Stone Age feet through an unfettered, exalted Eden. It was a land where nature ruled and man shrank from its fury or basked in plenty at the dictates of mysterious and awesome forces. Every creation of "He who gives breath" was in abundance; even the soil and rock seemed to have life. Imagination can recreate a partial view of this magical, holy wilderness, but no place remains on the continent to give an approximate comparison. But still, in the deeper recesses of hollows, or along a few windswept horizons, an enfolding, soothing caress of that favored land can be touched and felt, and with it, a sense of benevolent guardian spirits in the air and vibrating springs. On this hallowed ground it is even possible for modern wayfarers to rediscover the ancient reverence and oneness with the flowing mountainscape, to embrace and protect the diminished natural world which now recoils from the harsh, unrestrained hands of men.

Battle of the Stone Giants

In the old times, as far as can be traced back to the forefathers, some men had good luck and others had none. Likewise, some people are liked and revered for themselves, while others are shunned for no fault of their own. Why these inconsistencies exist are some of the secrets of the Master of Life.

Sometimes there are reasons we can't see:

Once there were two Seneca youths who lived in a very poor village in the deep forest. This was long ago, before the people learned to be charitable and share with those in need. The youths were constantly turned away from the lodges of their neighbors and kin and barely had enough food to stay alive. They came to rely only on each other. But, the closer they became the more they were disliked and neglected by others. When they were old enough, they decided to leave the rejection and abuse they had known and seek friendlier people and lands. They had no provisions and had no idea which direction to head, but they trusted the powers that give structure to life to watch over them.

At first they nearly starved to death, but they learned to make bows and arrows to hunt small game. After leaving the dense woods they came to marshy ground, but they still kept going. Occasionally one would say to the other, "I am afraid we shall never get through this rough place," but his companion would encourage him, and on they would go.

One day they came to a large hemlock tree. "Climb up and look around," said one; "See if there are any people in sight." The limbs of the tree came almost to the ground, hence he climbed it easily. From the top he saw a beautiful trail leading from the tree. "Throw down your bow and arrows and come up and see what a splendid trail I have found." The other went up, and looking at the trail, said, "Let us try it and see where it leads."

The trail proceeding from the tree seemed as solid as if on the earth, and it extended as far away as they could see. The young men traveled on without knowing that they were going up until they had reached another world, which seemed filled with game and was very pleasant. This was the domain of the powers that ruled the sun and moon and other natural forces under the watchful eyes of the Master of Life. The boys traveled for a long time in this enchanted upper world, receiving instructions as they went. Finally they met an old man who transformed and purified them so that they could enter the realm of departed spirits and the presence of the Master of Life.

They were given principles of religion and civilization and told to spread the message of kindness and charity among the people of their own country. The two travelers returned to earth and taught the wisdom and rules of right conduct. Their old village began to prosper and, seeing the benefits the new knowledge had brought, the two decided to travel to all the neighboring villages as well.

At length they said: "We have finished our work, for we have been over the entire land. We have spoken righteousness and justice to all the tribes of the north. Let us now turn to the tribes of the south." But, they didn't realize how difficult it would be to accomplish this goal.

On their journey toward the south they were constantly attacked by monsters with evil powers. They barely survived through the help of good spirits, but resolved to continue their quest. One evening they reached a bluff above a river and put up a little lodge. As one was building a fire the other went to look for game. The man making the fire could hear someone talking very loudly, as though making a speech. Going in the direction of the sound, he peered cautiously over the rims to see the speaker in the valley below. There were many people, and in the center on an elevated place, stood the speaker, who said: "Tomorrow we start on the trail leading to the place from which the two men came. At the journey's end we shall have a great feast." The man listening then understood that these were actually the great cannibal monsters called Stone Coats by some and Stone Giants by others. Few had ever seen them without their stone armor and lived to tell it.

When the hunter returned he also peeped over the hill and was so frightened he said, "We must hurry home." They knew that the Stone Coats intended to destroy them and eat all the inhabitants of their village. They went as far as they could that night, but the next day they heard the sound of the approach of the Stone Coats—the noise was like thunder.

The unusual stone formations of Judy Rocks in northeastern West Virginia

It was evident that they traveled faster than the two men, for when they camped that night the men were but a short distance ahead of them. The chief of the Stone Coats was heard saying, "Tomorrow we must be at the village." The faster of the two men, hastening to the village with a warning, said "The Stone Coats are coming and you shall surely die, but do not die without a struggle." He then returned to his comrade to face the danger. That night the invaders stopped to hunt and rest, and the Stone Coats chief said, "No one must go far; if he does and is away, he will lose his share of the feast." The two men could devise no way of saving themselves or their people. The people in the settlement were bewildered with fright and ran from place to place, not knowing what to do. The Stone Coats were near the village, when the chief said, "Let us halt and rest a little."

All at once the two friends saw a man with a smiling face, and when he came up, he said: "I will help you; I will save your people. I will conquer the Stone Coats, for the Master of Life has sent me to aid you." Telling the people who were running for their lives not to be alarmed if they heard a frightful noise, then, still smiling, he went down the bank into the valley where the Stone Coat army had halted to rest. Soon a terrible noise was heard, as of a desperate battle,

Eroding sedimentary stone of the Red River Gorge, eastern Kentucky, reveals patterns of an ancient ocean floor.

and steam could be seen rising above the hill from the sweat of the Stone Coats. Then the sounds came only at intervals and were not so loud, and finally they ceased altogether. The watchers saw the stranger with the smiling face coming back up the hill. He said: "I am thankful that I have destroyed them. The Stone Coats are all dead, and the people now alive will live in peace. I am appointed by the Master of Life to open the way and the paths to his people on earth. Wherever there is sorcery among your people, I am always sent against it and we are sure to kill all we pursue. I am the one you always call Lightning or Thunder."

The two friends then went to the place where the Stone Coat army had been. Only piles of stone remained. The stones found all over the earth are remains of this great battle and the killing of the Stone Giants. Thus, it was through the two transformed young men that the forefathers of the Senecas were saved from death and received their religion. They foretold what was to be as it is today, and their teachings are still honored.

—*Erminnie A. Smith*
Myths of the Iroquois, 1883

Northern West Virginia, including the areas overlooked by Spruce Knob, was once the domain of the Seneca tribe, one of the nations of the Iroquois League. They were known as the "People of the great mountains." Although distantly related, they were traditional enemies of the Cherokee. They claimed all the territory south to the Tennessee River Valley, and the Cherokee claimed all the lands north to the Ohio River. Both groups had many beliefs in common, including the high rank of the "Thunder Spirits" in their pantheon of beneficial beings.

According to local folklore, probably of recent vintage, the daughter of the band's head man devised an unusual plan for selecting her mate:

Princess Snowbird, daughter of Chief Bald Eagle and White Rock, grew up along the upper Potomac River in the shadow of the rocky formations known as "Seneca Rocks" and was the first person to ever climb to the tops of the pinnacles. Due to her great beauty and succession rights for her husband to become chief, she had many suitors. Sitting atop the summit one day, she decided she would marry the man brave enough to follow her along the dangerous paths up the mountain. Seven of the tribe's braves accepted her challenge and followed her as she ventured up the treacherous course. During the climb some of the braves fell to their deaths and others became discouraged and turned back. Nearing the summit she looked back to find that only one of her suitors had managed to reach the goal, but just below the top he slipped and was about to fall from the peak. Snowbird caught his hand and pulled him to safety. From that time the lovers were always seen sitting together on the heights dreaming and planning their lives. Their spirits still overlook their beloved valley from the mountain spires and their secret paths along the ridges.

The rocky summit of West Virginia's highest peak, Spruce Knob

The Warrior Maiden: Origin of Honeysuckle and Woodbine

In ancient times the Oneida ranged from the rivers and great lakes of the north country to the Cumberland and Tennessee regions. But due to a protracted war with their old enemies, the Mingo tribe, whose numbers were like the grains of sand, the once proud nation was reduced to a few old men, women and children. Still the Mingo would not leave them in peace and completely devastated their country, destroying their crops and homes. It was their practice to kidnap and adopt the younger women and children into their bands and kill and scalp all others they were able to find, until it seemed that even the name of the Oneida would be erased from the earth.

The small group that had survived retreated to the high bluffs in the deep forest, but even here they were not safe, since there were Mingo war parties constantly looking for them. The refugees couldn't forage for roots and berries or light a fire for warmth or to cook for fear that the smoke would be seen. The dilemma seemed to be that they could hide among the high cliffs and starve to death or be captured and killed by their tormenters. The people prayed to the One Above for help, but their situation appeared to be hopeless. But one night the Master of Things appeared in a dream to one young girl named Aliquipiso and told her how she might save her people.

The next morning all the people were called together and she told them of her vision and instructed them in all that they must do. After the people set about their task, Aliquipiso left the mountain sanctuary and began to wander through the woods as if looking for food. Soon captured by Mingo scouts, she was immediately taken to their camp where she was interrogated and tortured. She was told that if she would reveal the hiding place of her clan that her life would be spared and she would be adopted into the great Mingo nation. She refused all offers and bravely endured the abuse of her captors, impressing them with her stubbornness and endurance Finally, near the end of the day, she began to weaken and told them she could stand it no longer; she would lead them to the mountain haven.

She was warned that if she tried to betray them that they would kill her instantly, and the army set out through the forest following her along secret trails to the hiding place. As dark was approaching, they came to the base of a high cliff and Aliquipiso motioned silently to all the enemy warriors to gather near her, as if to point out the remaining course. With all the warriors gathered about her she suddenly signaled to her relatives on the bluffs above and they hurled the stones and boulders that they had spent the day amassing onto those below. In the resulting avalanche the entire enemy force was buried.

The remaining Mingos were so demoralized by the loss of their warriors that they retreated to the narrow valleys and mountains of what became West Virginia, and the Oneidas were left in peace and eventually grew to become one of the five nations of the Iroquois League. Aliquipiso had given her life to save her people. To commemorate her courage the Breathgiver caused woodbine, which is considered a good medicine, to grow from her hair. From her body sprang the honeysuckle which perfumes the forest in summer and it is called "Blood of brave women".

—based on Oneida legend
recorded in 1902 by W.W. Canfield

The Mingo Tribe

The Mingo tribe claimed all of what is now southern West Virginia as their hunting grounds. They were probably related to the Shawnee groups in the Ohio river region. One of the tribe's better known leaders was chief Logan who had many white friends of power and influence.

In 1774, at the beginning of Lord Dunmor's War, while treaties were being negotiated with the Indians, a drunken soldier killed all of Logan's family. This violation of the truce precipitated the Battle of Point Pleasant, a preamble to the American Revolution.

Lord Dunmor called a meeting of his officers and the various tribal delegates. Logan was conspicuous by his absence, and Chief Cornstalk was sent to request him to attend. Logan declined the invitation but sent a letter by Cornstalk to the council. It was a letter of a lonely, broken-hearted man. Cited by Thomas Jefferson in his **Notes of Virginia**, it became popular in churches and schools of the period:

''I appeal of any white man to say if ever he entered Logan's cabin hungry, and he gave not meat; if ever he came cold and naked, and he clothed him not. During the last and bloody war, Logan remained quiet in his cabin, an advocate of peace. Such was my love for the whites that my countrymen pointed as they passed and said, 'Logan is a friend of white men.' I had ever thought to have lived with you, but for the injuries of one man who the last spring, in cold blood, and unprovoked, murdered all the relatives of Logan, not even sparing my woman and children. There runs not a drop of my blood in the veins of any living creature. Who is there to mourn for Logan? Not one.''

Sky Bridge in Kentucky's Red River Gorge

The White Roots of Peace

Deganawidah was the Iroquois' legendary Law Giver and, with the assistance of his spokesman Hiawatha, is credited with the unification of the five nations of the Iroquois League. As in much of oral tradition, he was given magical powers in the sagas. He probably lived around the 15th century but could have been based on a composite of ancient tribal chiefs.

The five original tribes of the Iroquois League were the Mohawks, Oneidas, Onondagas, Cayugas and Senecas. The Tuscaroras joined to make the sixth after their defeat by combined colonial and Cherokee forces in 1710. They were sometimes allied with the Shawnee and Delaware against their southern and eastern neighbors.

The Great White Pine was their symbol for a sheltering tree of peace, which might extend to embrace all of mankind under it branches, with the white roots of peace reaching the four quarters of the earth.

Deganawidah was sent by the Great Master of Life to bring peace and stop the shedding of blood between human beings. On leaving home he told his mother and grandmother that he would never return, but if they wished to know how his mission had gone, they should go to the top of a nearby hill where a single tree stood, cut at the tree with their hatchets, and if blood flowed from the wound, they would know He had perished and His work had failed.

At that time the Iroquois lived in remote, stockaded villages hidden in the hills and were weak before the raids of their Algonquin enemies, as the Adirondacks and Mahicans. The laws handed down by Deganawidah were based on principles of reason, righteousness, justice, health and peace. Consensus was to be gained through long debate and contemplation in council. Through a representative form of government, open to all, the rule of law was certain and peace and tranquillity prevailed. Their joint action made them a dominant force throughout the colonial period and survives today on their reservations. Their idea of hunting grounds held in common may account for the vast uninhabited valleys between the Blue Ridge and Cumberland mountains that drew a surge of settlers in the decade preceding the American Revolution.

The fighting strength of the Iroquois League was broken in 1784, but many of its ideals live in the influence it had on framers of the American republic. Their accomplishment was recognized by Benjamin Franklin and Thomas Jefferson in their writings and speeches.

Many Iroquois chroniclers skip over Deganawidah and attribute the heroic deeds to Hiawatha. In these epics Atotarho was the giant with the marvelous hair, which consisted of living snakes, and he became a great wizard. Additional sagas tell how Hiawatha sacrificed his beloved daughter Minnihaha to the Great Mystery to maintain tranquillity, strengthen tribal bonds and to prevail over rival groups. In the following story Deganawidah plays the interchangeable role of the great unifier and lawgiver.

How Hiawatha was Transformed from a Beast to a Prophet

Deganawidah had great magical powers and set out on his odyssey to bring tranquillity to humankind in a white stone canoe that seemed to glide in a radiant cloud across the waters. He amazed those he encountered along the shores with His wisdom and soon had many followers. But the forest along the rivers and lakes were dangerous places to travel. In addition to enemy war parties that had forced the tribes of the region to hide in the mountains from their oppressors, the woods were also the haunt of a superhuman cannibal whose hair was a mass of snakes.

The roar of this monster in the forest struck terror into the hearts of even the bravest who heard it. Although the first tribe Deganawidah met on his mission liked his prophecy, they said there could be no peace as long as the cannibal carried off their people. But their chief was a brave man and he followed Deganawidah's instructions to go meet with the monster.

Of course, the cannibal promptly hit the peace delegate on the head and mindlessly carried him off to his cabin to cook the chief for supper. Unknown to the monster, Deganawidah had climbed onto the roof of his lodge and placed his face over the smoke hole above the fireplace and lay looking down over the cannibal's shoulder. Filling his

View from the John Muir Trail in the Big South Fork National Recreation Area near the Tennessee/Kentucky border

giant pot with water, the cannibal set it into the fireplace to cook his meal but paused in his preparations to gaze at the image reflected on the mirrored surface.

"Wait," he thought, "I never realized what a wise and gentle face I had. This is not the face of a man who would terrorize his neighbors and attack strangers in the forest." At first he couldn't believe his eyes and kept going back to look at the reflection. But it was true, the face that looked back at him was one of great wisdom and kindness, and this started the monster to thinking. As he thought, his nature and even appearance began to change. And the more he thought the more he realized how his life of violence must be changed and that from that day onward he would use his great power for good and help mankind find the ways of peace.

He released his prisoner, and the chief combed the serpents out of his hair. His evil form had been changed to one of wisdom and beneficence, and he became spokesman for Deganawidah, the Great Law Giver. His name, revered by generations of Iroquois, was Hiawatha.

*—Based on versions by Paul A.W. Wallace, **The White Roots of Peace**, 1946, and Erminnie A. Smith, **Myths of the Iroquois**, 1883.*

The Legendary Mike Fink

The exploits of Mike Fink were more fanciful than real. As new waves of immigrants crossed the mountains and the frontier moved westward, rivers such as the Tennessee, Cumberland and Ohio became the highways along which both goods and people moved. Fink was probably born near present day Pittsburgh around 1770 and was killed in a quarrel on the Missouri River around 1822.

Numerous anecdotes floated up and down the Ohio and Mississippi watersheds about his adventures, growing with each telling, until he was reported to have superhuman and animal qualities. He bragged to his fellow keel-boatmen:

"Well, I walk tall into varmint and Indian, it's a way I've got, and it comes as natural as grinning to a hyena. I'm a regular tornado, tough as a hickory withe, long winded as a nor'-wester. I can strike a blow like a falling tree, and every lick makes a gap in the crowd that lets in an acre of sunshine. Whew, boys!"

—*Thomas Bangs Thorpe*
The Disgraced Scalp Lock, *1842*

Fink is frequently painted as a crude and unsavory character, scoffing at the law and rights of others, as in the following story:

How Mike Fink Came to Court at Louisville

In all his little tricks, as Mike called them, he never displayed any respect for the laws either of propriety or property, but he was so ingenious in his predations that it is impossible not to laugh at his crimes. The stern vigor of Justice, however, did not feel disposed to laugh at Mike, but on the contrary offered a reward for his capture. For a long time he could not be arrested, until an old friend of his, who happened to be a constable, came to him asking that he allow himself to be taken, so he could collect the reward. Pleading the poverty of his family, and presuming on Mike's kind heart, the constable told him that it was very unlikely that he would be convicted. Mike allowed the constable to serve the warrant, but, since he and his men didn't feel at home anywhere except on their boat, with the condition that they and their craft should be carried to the courthouse.

A long wagon was procured with oxen to carry it from the river. In early days as a frontier outpost, Louisville's streets were still little more than dirt ruts, and the route was very steep and muddy. Regardless of this, however, the boat was set upon the wagon, and Mike and his men, with their long poles ready, as if for an aquatic excursion, began the trip. By dint of laborious dragging the wagon had attained half the height of the hill, when Mike called out to his men—"Set Poles!" and the end of every long pole was set firmly in the thick mud—"Back Her!" roared Mike from the stern, and back down the hill went wagon, yawl, men, and oxen. Mike had been revolving the matter in his mind and had concluded that it was best not to go; and well knowing that each of his men was equal to a moderately strong ox, he had at once conceived and executed his retrograde movement.

After another parley at the bottom of the hill he was persuaded to continue the journey, and back up the hill the procession rolled. This time they had almost reached the top of the hill, when "Set Poles—Back Her" was again ordered and executed. A third attempt, however, was successful and Mike and his men reached the courthouse in safety. As his friend had sworn, he was acquitted for lack of sufficient evidence. Other indictments were then found against him, but Mike preferred not to wait to hear them tried; so, at a given signal, he and his men boarded their craft and weighed anchor. Dread of the long poles in the hands of Mike's men prevented the posse from delaying their departure. As they left the courthouse yard Mike waved his red bandanna and, promising to "call again", was borne back to his element and launched once more upon the waters.

—*Retold from Ben Casseday,*
The History of Louisville...

Autumn colors are reflected in the Big South Fork of the Cumberland River, near the Tennessee/Kentucky border.

...everything in nature called destruction must be creation — a change from beauty to beauty.
                              —John Muir, 1911

The Mystery of the Melungeons

Origins of the unusual clans called "Melungeons" by the white settlers who first encountered them, living in the isolated ridges and hollows along the eastern slopes of the Cumberlands, will probably remain as illusive as the cities of gold that Desoto sought on his ill fated journey. The mountain fastness has guarded their secrets well. And while prospectors uncovered part of the lode sought by the Spanish, three centuries later in hills of northern Georgia and western North Carolina, less solid evidence is known about these mountaineers. All that seems certain is that settlers moving into the narrow valleys of the Clinch River watershed and throughout the Cumberlands found another people established there who were neither White nor Indian.

In dress, farming and housing customs they were very similar to the pioneers, but they had no written titles to their farms and were pushed out to the less desirable hill and ridge sides. Early census records place their numbers at perhaps 30,000 souls, diffused along the mountains of northeastern Tennessee, eastern Kentucky, southwest Virginia and parts of West Virginia. Generations of assimilation by the larger population has erased most of the traits that identified these "Mountain People," as their descendants prefer to be called. This is a trait shared with most Indian groups, since they simply called themselves "The People" or "The Principle People," and the name given the tribe, frequently by their enemies, had no meaning in their language. There are few families with ties to the frontier that don't list on their family trees, and usually with pride, at least a few of their red brothers or sisters, or perhaps a Melungeon or two.

Substantial speculation has been offered on the origins of the group, ranging from exotic to mundane. Some of these theories are:

They were descended from Phoenician sailors shipwrecked along the North Carolina outerbanks and pushed inland by hostile natives. Support for this idea comes from the mediterranean features of many of the group, and their stature and complexions are different from neighboring bands. It has also been claimed that some had old Roman coins in their possession and "melungeon" could be derived from words for shipmate.

Another theory makes the case that they are descended from deserters and Portuguese conscripts of DeSoto, or later secret Spanish expeditions, who hid out in the mountains with friendly natives. It is unknown how many of the 600 men who left Florida in 1540 looking for gold with DeSoto joined tribes along the way, but several desertions were recorded in their journals, and only about half the group finished the journey.

Other theories give them a north European background, citing the extensive wanderings of the Vikings, and also a Welsh legend of Prince Madoc. According to Welsh folklore, this second son sought to establish himself in the lands to the west, and set sail from Wales in the mid-ages. He returned with glowing accounts of the country he had visited on his voyage and took several ships of immigrants with him to establish a colony, and was never heard from again.

Indian tradition tells of a strange race of white people with blue eyes residing in the foothills. They warred constantly with surrounding tribes until they were forced to sue for peace and withdrew to the west. In another account, a Welsh minister claimed to be released by Indians that were about to kill him when he recognized they were speaking his native language, and when he responded in Gaelic, he was greeted as a brother. These legends sparked the curiosity of ethnologists during the last century, and at least one survey of western tribes was made seeking these immigrants, but without success.

Less exotic theories place the Melungeon among groups described as "Tri-Racial Isolates" that retreated into remote regions during the Indian removal or earlier. It was common for white traders and hunters to forsake their European ties and adopt Indian ways during the era before farmers began pouring across the Blue Ridge. They married into the tribes and some of their offspring became noted warriors against later white encroachment. This process apparently took place in the establishment of the Chickamauga towns that split off from the main Cherokee tribe. They continued to harass travelers along the Tennessee River long after the main tribe had been subdued. These may have also been joined by an occasional runaway slave and other renegade whites and dispossessed Indians. The upper Clinch was thinly settled until after the Civil War but was notorious as a haven for outlaws from the time of the Revolution.

South Arch stands amid the rhododendron, hickory and hemlock in the Big South Fork National Recreation Area in northern Tennessee.

Mount Rogers Area

Once these mountains were part of overlapping tribal hunting ranges claimed by the Cherokee, Monacan, Tuscarora, Delaware and other Algonquin and Iroquois related groups.

According to the migration lore of the Cherokee, Delaware and Iroquois, the Cherokee had once lived much farther north than the land occupied at the arrival of white explorers. It is probable that they once lived along the Ohio River basin but suffered a major defeat at the hands of the Delawares, Senecas and allied Iroquois. They were then pushed south and east along the watersheds of the New and Kanawah Rivers, through West Virginia, and into Virginia. They resided for a time in the region of the Peaks of Otter, but through the generations, due to continuing wars, following game or to replenish spent farm land, the loosely related groups moved south along the Holston and Tennessee Rivers to occupy the foothills regions of Tennessee, North Carolina, South Carolina and Georgia at the arrival of the settlement era. They maintained disputed claims for an even wider territory, including parts of Alabama and Kentucky. During the colonial period large Cherokee contingents and hunting parties were reported as far north as the Falls of the James River, present day Richmond. Bitter intertribal warfare continued throughout the colonial period, and the Cherokee played major rolls in the dispossession of their traditional adversaries. The eventual removal of most native American groups from their traditional homes is a long, sad and complex story in which neither white nor red man looks very good.

High atop the Iron Mountains that stand between the Blue Ridge and Cumberland Chains, there are several pinnacles, known locally as Buzzard Knob, Buzzard Point and the like. Commanding sweeping panoramas of the folding blue-green landscape, eagles, buzzards and other large hunting fowl once launched themselves from these vantage points to soar for hours on rising thermal currents and cast long menacing shadows into the valleys they surveyed for game or carrion.

The eagle was universally revered by the Indians and was thought to have magical powers. Its feathers were used as marks of bravery and in tribal dances and rituals. Only certain hunters, familiar with the special formulas, could kill an eagle, and they were employed to obtain their feathers. After fasting, meditation and invoking mystical guidance, the hunter would place a freshly killed deer on a high point, then conceal himself until the eagle came to the bait.

Buzzards were also thought to have special influence that could be called on for success in hunting. The Great Buzzard, ancient father of all the birds, played a prominent roll in the Genesis traditions of many Woodlands Nations including the Cherokee, Creek and Yuchi.

Prominent features of the Virginia Highlands are the Appalachian Balds. These open, grassy meadows, interspersed with heath bogs, rhododendron gardens, shrubs and various berry thickets, once stretched along the high summits the length of the Blue Ridge chain. Many explanations have been offered for how these peaks, all well below the altitude that trees usually dominate, came to be bald. However they came to be, they are rapidly disappearing along with their unique ecological systems and rare plant varieties. In this area many of the open balds have been preserved by grazing livestock, including a small, free roaming, pony herd released to fend for themselves after the market for mine ponies collapsed.

One mythical explanation of how the balds were created comes from the Cherokee:

How the Appalachian Balds Came to Be

A monstrous flying creature, resembling a great winged hornet and the size of a house, once terrorized the people who lived in the Nantahala region near present day Franklin, North Carolina. Without warning it would swoop down and carry off young children if they wandered into the woods alone or strayed far from their mothers. It got to be such a problem that they decided to declare war on the menace. After several unsuccessful attempts to kill it, the work was turned over to their medicine men to devise a plan to eliminate the beast.

Somehow the beast would have to be traced to its lair and killed there. But because it had always eluded them when it was chased, it was decided that they would station

Snow covers the meadows and fir trees atop Whitetop Mountain, above Buzzard Rock, in the area called "Virginia's Rooftop".

themselves on all the highest peaks, and when one spotted the monster, the alarm was spread by "Halloo's" from summit to summit. In this way they finally traced the beast to a deep cavern at the head of the Tugaloo River in South Carolina. Unfortunately, the place was inaccessible to human feet, and it looked as if their efforts would lead to frustration again. But the warriors prayed to the Great Spirit to force the creature out of its den so that they could get at it with their weapons.

He had the Great Thunders send a terrible storm and a stroke of lightning which tore away half of the mountain, and the Indians were able to destroy the monster.

The Great Spirit was so pleased by the courage shown by the Cherokees in the battle that he willed that all the highest mountains in their land should thereafter be destitute of trees so they would always be able to watch the movements of their enemies.

> —based on account by Charles Lanman
> ***Letters from the Allegheny Mountains***, 1849

Other versions of this story place the site of the monster's den in other locations and state that the beast was actually a great Yellow Jacket, father of all the yellow jackets today. It has also been speculated that the fiery explosion witnessed by the Indians was actually an ancient volcanic eruption on one of the high peaks.

Trout lilies, named because of the mottled pattern of their leaves, bloom in the Mount Rogers National Recreation Area of Virginia.

The coneflower, blackeyed susan and trout lilly were all called ''Deer eye'' due to their shapes and were used in eye related treatments in folk medicine.

Ferns abound on the Appalachian Balds of the Grayson Highlands along the Appalachian Trail in the Rhododendron Gap Area of the Mount Rogers National Recreation Area of Virginia.

A variety of ferns were used in folk remedies. Due to the way the young shoots unfurl, it was thought to be beneficial in the treatment of rheumatism.

Dogwood berries stand in relief during an early winter snowstorm beside Watauga Lake in northeastern Tennessee.

Origin of the Evergreens

A long time ago, when the world was new, the Giver of Breath called all the creatures together to fast and meditate. He instructed all the plants and animals to remain in their townhouses and to reflect on the nature of things, but no one was to go to sleep for seven days.

Some of the creatures tried hard, but just couldn't keep their eyes open and went fast asleep the very first night. In spite of their good intentions, as the week passed one nodded off and then another, until all but a handful had given up the vigil. On the eighth morning the

Grass and leaves are frozen in pools near Bradley Gap in western North Carolina.

Master of Things returned to see who had obeyed His wishes. As punishment for those plants that had not observed his request, He decreed that they would wither and die at autumn or lose their leaves during the winter. The plants that had endured through the vigil became the Evergreens such as the cedar, fir, rhododendron, holly and pine, and they were given special spiritual powers. For the animals that had persisted He gave the gift of being able to see and hunt at night while the others groped around in the dark.

—*Retold from James Mooney*
Myths of the Cherokee

Hump Mountain, Yellow Mountain, and Roan Highlands areas

"God Is Nigh"

The high treeless balds of the Appalachians are places of enchantment and mystery. Why these ridges are not forested is a subject of speculation since they were clear before written or oral records. Initially they were probably cleared by fire, either natural or man-made, then kept open by burning and by browsing animals.

The open Appalachian Balds harbor unique ecological systems that have developed over centuries. The Roan Highlands, which include Roan Mountain, Grassy Ridge Bald, Big and Little Yellow Mountains and Big and Little Hump Mountains, support more natural flowering species than any other part of the temperate zones. A kaleidoscope of colors greets hikers throughout the warm months. But these open leas, used as pasture following the displacement of the Indians, are rapidly shrinking since the impact of grazing stock and wildlife has been greatly reduced. Most of the Bald Mountains, so named for the expanse of mountaintops to the north and south which were once clear, are not bald anymore.

The Appalachian Bald is a special place. Rare shrubs and wildflowers serve as anchors for less tangible, spiritually uplifting sensations within this realm of light. In contrast, enfolding forest and hollows surround the wayfarer with a sense of closeness on lower ridges. Breaking out into the open, bright, airy vistas gives a perception of soaring exhilaration amid the drifting clouds and unlimited horizons after passing softly upon a heavy pile carpet of leaves and dark humus in the mist-laden hollows, rich with moss and ferns where even the air seems to vibrate with emerald hues.

These grassy peaks are homes of the "Immortals", the Nunnehi of the Cherokee, a race of spirit people. Normally they are invisible but, if they want to, they can appear as ordinary people. They might appear to help wanderers lost in the mountains or aid their chosen against enemies. Friendly spirits, they are fond of music and dancing, and they may be heard in the lonely places among high ridges. But the highlands are also home to the fairy-like Yunwi Tsunsdi or "Little People". Their tracks are sometimes found in the snow or in soft ground around springs and may lead to rocky shelters or caves in the hills. They are also kindhearted, cheerful people spending half their time dancing and drumming and are great wonder workers. Two of these little fellows are Tsawasi and Tsagasi. Both are good natured but, like leprechauns, may also be mischievous. The first of them is very handsome, with long hair falling down to his feet, and lives in grassy patches on the hillsides. He has great power over the game, and if his spirit is invoked by the hunter, he will have the skill to slip up on the deer through the long grass without being seen. His companion can also give the hunter extra powers, but is more tricky. When someone trips or falls, it may be Tsagasi who has caused it. Some say that the spirit people left following the Indian Removals in 1838,

Winter view of Yellow and Hump Mountains along the Tennessee/North Carolina border

An early winter snowstorm blankets the Roan Highlands in this view from Little Hump Mountain along the Tennessee/North Carolina border.

but others claim that in the Bald Mountains the ancient spirits can still be heard around dusk, and sometimes their campfires spotted on distant slopes.

The high balds are a magically bright and cheerful world with waving grasses, brilliant beds of rhododendron and azalea and prolific blackberry and blueberry bushes. But the mood can change dramatically, and within minutes, to dark and eerie with damp clouds looming above and raking the passes. Prevailing winds sculpt the shrubs and dwarf trees into gnarled masses, hovering like gnomes along the paths and collecting hoarfrost and ice in the winter.

Walking in solitude along the spine of these haunting crests can invoke reveries of a timeless Appalachia. These exalted meadows have witnessed the passing of Stone Age nomads, long forgotten Indian war parties, and the

Ferns, snakeroot, asters and other wildflowers cover the forest floor at Yellow Mountain Gap, near the junction to the Appalachian and Overmountain Victory Trails.

struggles of immigrant pioneers. Still they offer a refuge beneath the Great Apportioner of Time, the Sun (deputy of the Giver of Breath), as He watches over the world and a temporary haven from a world of spreading chaos. Following the footsteps and passing souls of ten millennia, wayfarers seeking a gentle perspective may still call on the stewards of high shining paths for peace and harmony. Nowhere are the ancient spirits nearer.

Yellow Mountain Gap stands on the crest of the Iron Mountains along the imaginary line that divides Tennessee and North Carolina. This high passage was the main route of aboriginal hunters, traders and warriors across the mountains. In 1670 a German traveler, John Ledner, possibly crossed this point in his journey along the borders of the Cherokee country. His route is not known, but he reported that his Indian guides fell to the ground to pray when they saw the Blue Ridge chain on the horizon, a view similar to those offered from these high summits, and proclaimed that "God is Nigh".

The trail across the gap was a wide swath worn deep by passing feet and migrating wildlife herds. This was one of the routes followed by Daniel Boone in his explorations across the mountains.

Today's view across the open balds and forested ridges surveys much the same scene witnessed by aboriginal warriors as they paused to conjure against their enemies and seek the help of the immortals. The divide was also the route (for a time known as Brights Trace) taken by thousands of emigrants, as they passed from the safety of their known world to the certain hardships of the backwater regions to the west. Travel today is restricted to foot and animal traffic at this junction of the Appalachian Trail and the Overmountain Victory Trail, as it has been for centuries.

The Overmountain Men

The Overmountain Victory Trail commemorates the route taken by frontier fighters from recently established Watauga, Holston and Nolichuckey area

This view across the open meadows at Yellow Mountain Gap on the Tennessee/North Carolina border is similar to the scene that greeted ancient nomads and pioneer travelers.

settlements to join other patriots in the decisive defeat of loyalist troops at Kings Mountain, South Carolina, in 1780. This battle has been called the turning point in the Revolutionary War in the south. An early ankle-deep snowfall greeted the volunteers as they crossed the pass on foot and horseback. Superficially, this army of frontiersmen, gathered from the new settlements of east Tennessee and southwest Virginia, probably looked more like a ragtag, undisciplined mob, with no uniforms and few provisions. But their long rifles and fighting tactics, many adopted from the Indians, made them more than a match for English muskets and American Loyalist troops commanded by Major Patrick Ferguson. The volunteers were dressed in tasseled hunting shirts, beadwork belts and mink or coonskin caps. In Indian fashion, they stained their horses' trappings yellow and red and carried tomahawks and scalp-

A butterfly feeds on blooms of wild flame azalea on Yellow Mountain, on the Tennessee/North Carolina highlands.

ing knives—there was neither a bayonet nor tent in the army. Battle casualties in the British command were 1,018 compared with 92 on the Patriot side. Killed in the engagement, Ferguson was the only non-American on either side of the battle.

The Overmountain Men were a controversial band. Historians have called them heroes as well as scoundrels, merely protecting narrow self-interest. A popular image of these settlers, first to cross the barrier of mountains, is of land-starved refugees, displaced peasants and city poor. This identity probably applied to later waves of settlers better. During an era when literacy was uncommon among the working class, records of these settlements show that a large percentage, perhaps a majority, could read and write. Many had the means to establish and defend large land holdings. They owned herds of cattle and horses and even a few slaves. Some of the first attempts at self-government were established in their settlements, far from the coastal seats of power. Enlightened ideals, expressed in the Watauga Association, Cumberland Compact and

State of Franklin charters, indicate they were no mere ruffians.

Whatever their nature — grandiose entrepreneurs and land speculators or selfless benefactors of humanity — the vast regions they entered had been vacated; old Indian fields lined many of the river bottoms. The rich valleys had been cultivated and hunted over by a succession of Amerind groups for 10,000 years or longer. Evidence, such as arrowheads and pottery shards, of their long occupation is still turned over each year by plows, fulfilling the prophecy of the great Shawnee leader Tecumseh in a speech trying to unite all the Indian tribes to stop the settlement move west.

"…Where today is the Pequod? Where the Narragansetts, the Mohawks, Pocanokets, and many other once powerful tribes of our race? They have vanished before the avarice and oppression of the white men, as snow before a summer sun…. So it will be with you Choctaws and Chickasaws! Soon your mighty forest trees, under the shade of whose wide spreading branches you have played in infancy, sported in boyhood, and now rest your wearied limbs after the fatigue of the chase, will be cut down to fence in the land which the white intruders dare to call their own. Soon their broad roads will pass over the graves of your fathers, and the place of their rest will be blotted out forever. The annihilation of our race is at hand unless we unite in one common cause against the common foe. Think not, brave Choctaws and Chickasaws, that you can escape the common fate. Your people, too, will soon be as falling leaves and scattering clouds before their blighting breath. You, too, will be driven away from your native land and ancient domains as leaves are driven before the wintry storms….

"Will not the bones of our dead be plowed up, and their graves be turned into fields?…"

Catawba rhododendron are in peak bloom on Grassy Ridge Bald, looking toward the Highlands of Roan.

Catawba rhododendron blooms on Round Bald, Tennessee, near Carvers Gap.

How the Rhododendron Got Their Bright Colors

There are conflicting accounts of how the rhododendron, azalea and other wildflowers received their colors while others remained white. Two stories of how the Catawba Rhododendron got their colors follow:

Warriors of the Catawba tribe were renowed for their fierceness and fighting ability. One day they challenged all the neighboring nations who wished to seek revenge for the many rivals they had killed to join them in one final battle atop the high mountains to settle their grievances. At that time the mountaintops were covered with trees and all the shrubs were colorless or white.

Even the tribes without a grudge could not ignore such a dare once they heard it, and on the appointed day all the warriors in the region joined the battle. The fighting was so intense that everything on the crests, for as far as the eye

View southwest over the Roan Highlands from the junction of the Appalachian and Grassy Ridge Bald trails on the Tennessee/North Carolina border

could see, was knocked down. So much blood was spilled that thereafter the Catawba Rhododendron would always be stained in hues of red.

A happier account follows:

Early one evening the West Wind was out painting the colors in the sky, with rich magenta, purple and violet, to signal the day's end and perhaps the approach of fair weather. He had become accustomed to performing this duty in solitude along the remote crests, but this day he was startled to see a young maiden strolling along the ridges. He was so awed by her beauty that he forgot what he was doing and spilled his paints on the surrounding highlands. Until that time all the plants had blooms of white, but from that day until this the alpine rhododendron have the bright colors of the evening sky, while the azaleas caught the splattering flame yellows and scarlets of the setting sun.

Settlement Era

Daniel Boone was only one of a cadre of bigger-than-life heroes in buckskin of the Appalachian frontier. Their exploits, real or imagined, served as diversions from the hardships and dangers of pioneer life and were told, retold, and embellished around campfires and hearths far from the centers of civilization. Frequently, the name of the hero of a good yarn would change with the locale, and deeds attributed to Boone in North Carolina or Kentucky might be credited to Tom Quick in Pennsylvania or Mike Fink in Ohio. Attaining mythical status, the yarns became models for a rich oral tradition in the isolation of mountains where men were ''Half-horse, half-alligator, and a bit of snapping turtle'', with extraordinary skills at Indian fighting, marksmanship, and general bravado.

One account tells how Boone and his men, badly out-numbered by a band of marauding Indians, avoided a confrontation:

Boone's Knife-Swallowing Trick

Daniel Boone was once resting in the woods with his companions, when a large party of warriors came suddenly upon them. Both parties were surprised at encountering the other, and since Boone and his men were about to sit down to dinner, the Indians were invited to join them in their meal. Boone was suspicious of their intentions and told his men to keep their weapons at hand; the Indians pretended to be friendly while looking for them to let their guard down.

In the tension around the campfire, Boone swaggered unarmed over to the head man of the tribe, took the meat from the bone near them and rapidly downed it. He then ask to see the chief's scalping knife. The chief handed it to him without hesitation, and the pioneer, through sleight of hand, appeared to gulp down the knife with relish. The Indians were astonished. Rubbing his stomach with apparent satisfaction with the dessert, he pronounced it very good. After enjoying the surprise of the spectators for a few moments, he made some additional contortions and appeared to draw forth the knife and returned it to the baffled chief.

The chief tenuously felt the tip and blade of the knife, then tossed it into the bushes as if to avoid being contaminated. The Indians immediately retreated to the forest for fear that they may have come in contact with a great conjurer.

—*Charles McKnight*
***Our Western Border...,* 1876**

Boone's quick wits saved him from capture on many occasions; once he hid behind a waterfall to avoid detection. On another occasion, while splitting rails for a fence, he was surrounded by half a dozen braves. Seeing the futility of fighting, he told the Indians he would surrender and go with them peacefully, but that he hated to leave a job unfinished. The log he was working on had defied all his attempts to split it. If they would help him split the log, it could save them the work of subduing him. Of course the braves knew his reputation for gouging and hand to hand fighting, but they admired his cheek in the face of overwhelming odds and accepted his challenge.

To help him finish splitting the obstinate beam, he directed the Indians to each take one side of the rail in their hands and pull as hard as they could to rive the log to its end. Agreeing that this was the best strategy for dividing the stubborn rail, they grabbed the rail and, with Boone yelling cadence, began to heave in earnest. Intent on splitting the log, they momentarily took their eyes off Boone. He quickly grabbed his mall and knocked the wedge out of the log. The log instantly snapped shut like a steel trap, snaring his would-be assailants.

A story with more mystical overtones tells how Boone found his wife Rebecca:

Daniel Boone: How He Won Rebecca.

Daniel Boone, when a young man, was out on a ''Fire hunt'' with a companion in the dense forest of the Yadkin Valley of North Carolina. This type of night hunting, now illegal, takes advantage of the fact that deer and other wildlife freeze in their tracks, temporarily stunned or blinded, when a bright light is shined into their eyes. The

Flame azalea blooms with rhododendron along the Appalachian Balds of the Tennessee/North Carolina Highlands.

hunter's friend was preceding him with the "Fire pan", when all at once Boone quietly gave the signal to stop—an indication that he had "shined the eyes" of a deer. He crept cautiously forward—his rifle at the ready—and, sure enough: there were two liquid orbs turned full upon him.

Boone raised his rifle to shoot, but something mysterious held him back. Off sprang the startled game with a bound and a rustle and the ardent young hunter in hot pursuit. On! on! they ran; when, lo and behold! a fence appeared, over which the nimble deer vaulted with ease, while Boone, burdened with rifle and hunting gear, clambered after as best he could. In the distance he saw the house of Morgan Bryan and Boone said to himself, "I will chase this pet deer to its covert," and so, fighting his way though a score of snarling hounds, he knocked at the door, and was admitted and welcomed by farmer Bryan. The young hunter, panting from his exertions, had scarce time to throw his eyes about inquiringly, before a boy of ten, and a flushed and breathless girl of sixteen, with ruddy cheeks, flaxen hair and soft blue eyes, rushed into the room.

"Oh, father! father!" cried the boy. "Sis was down to the creek to set my lines, and was chased by a 'painter' (panther) or something. She's to skeared to tell." The "painter" and "deer" were now engaged in exchanging glances, and apparently the eyes of both had been most effectually "shined," and that is how Rebecca Bryan became Rebecca Boone.

—*Charles McKnight*
***Our Western Border...**, 1876*

On the flame Azalea—

...the blossoms cover the shrubs in such incredible profusion on the hillsides, that suddenly opening to view from dark shades, we are alarmed with the apprehension of the hills being set on fire. This is certainly the most gay and brilliant flowering shrub yet known...

—William Bartram, 1775
The Travels of William Bartram

The high crests of the Iron and Black Mountains stand like islands above the clouds in this view west from Unaka Mountain in the Pisgah/Cherokee National Forest.

I beheld with rapture and astonishment, a sublimely awful scene of power and magnificence, a world of mountains piled upon mountains.

—William Bartram, 1775
The Travels of William Bartram

Grays lily blooms amid ferns and golden hawkweeds in the unique ecology of the Appalachian Balds of the Roan Highlands on the Tennessee/North Carolina border.

Laurel Fork Falls in spring in the Cherokee National Forest of northeast Tennessee

The Long Man

There is another world under this, and it is like ours in everything—animals, plants, and people—save that the seasons are different. We know that the seasons are reversed because streams are warmer in winter than the air and cooler in the summer. The streams that come down from the mountains are the trails by which we reach this underworld, and the springs at their heads are the doorways by which we enter it, but to do this one must fast and go to water and have one of the underground people for a guide.

—*Retold from James Mooney*
***Myths of the Cherokee**, 1900*

Waterfalls are places of renewal and retreat from an encroaching mechanical world. Their constant drumming focuses a pure flow of vibrations to create one of the forest's most powerful mantras, and they blot out competing thoughts and sounds. Places of mystery and pilgrimage, their allure crosses the generations as abodes of ''Thunder spirits'' who speak through never ceasing murmurs and roars to those who seek their help.

Waterfalls do seem to speak, sometimes in a voice that is a deep rumbling bass and in other moments with twinkling high clefs. Every bump and crevice along the throat of the torrent adds some inflection or reverberation, altering tone or pitch, and creates a chorus of innumerable voices from the compression and expansion of air before the rush of falling water. This timbre is in continuous flux as the volume of water rises and falls, and each rolling pebble or leaf contributes its small note to the grand symphony. The range of these natural orchestras may rise from gentle whispers to frantic, pounding crescendos.

Sounds reflecting through this damp, forested domain evoke images of monks and shamans chanting A-U-M, half a world away; images of ancient medicine men and souls close to nature's secrets seeking spiritual oneness, or the deeper meanings of the journey of time and life; images of the ancients bathed in a misty, diffused light and echoes of past centuries; and images of transitory spirits pausing before the sound and energy of the universe, common to all, in the endless, random, unfathomable journey, from birth to death, from mountain springs to the sea. A-U-M, surrounding, A-U-M, permeating all within the emerald alpine niche, A-U-M, blending wandering spirits and worlds across an abyss of time. The cascades and tumbling creeks of the Appalachian Mountains are natural generators of alpha waves, recognized as beneficial in research into biofeedback and the effects of meditation, in this non-linear domain, where no two droplets ever take exactly the same course in their journeys.

Autumn leaves collect in the pool below Laurel Fork Falls in northeast Tennessee.

Ancient myths tell of thunder spirits that inhabit all the cliffs and mountains, especially in caves behind the great waterfalls. These beings travel around their domain along invisible bridges and arches throughout the highlands. Many are friendly, helpful spirits, but darker phantom beings responsible for mischief, discord and danger might also reside there.

Danger is present; a perpetual misting of oxygen and nutrient-laden spray promotes the growth of algae and mosses along the streams and treacherous footing for the unwary.

In Indian lore the rivers and creeks of the mountains were frequently referred to as "The Long Man", since this animated being was linked from the falling rains to the distant seas.

Cascading streams through remote mountain hollows may conceal the edges of another world. Listen the next time you walk along a tumbling branch. Just behind the obvious splashing and rush of water falling over boulders, there is another sound. The sound of tom-toms can be heard distinctly in places, faintly in others. In remote hollows the drums are amplified to the point that they dominate other sounds and seem to be joined by laughter and perhaps dancing nearby. This exercise requires no imagination, just a quiet moment of contemplation to hear the undertone of the forest.

Crabtree Falls, reached by a one-and-one-half-mile trail from the Blue Ridge Parkway in western North Carolina

Rock Creek Falls in northeast Tennessee, reached by a two-and-one-half-mile walk near the edge of the Unaka Mountain Wilderness Area

We…passed away the remaining part of the day in observing the beauties of the place…. As I was wandering about…embosomed in the woods and mountains, I could not but reflect what an insignificant creature I appeared among these magnificent works of the divine Creator.

—Francis Baily,
**Journal of a Tour in the Unsettled Parts of the
United States of North America in 1796 and 1797**

David Crockett

David Crockett was another of the frontier characters whose lives were amplified to the level of super men, of the half-alligator, half-horse and a bit of snapping turtle variety. Born in 1786 on the frontier, in today's Greene County, Tennessee, Crockett was a famous yarn spinner, marksman, hunter and Indian fighter. He served in the state legislature of Tennessee and in the Congress of the United States. He fought under Andrew Jackson in the defeat of the Creek tribe at the battle of Horseshoe Bend but eventually split with the President on treatment of the vanquished eastern tribes. He advocated fair treatment for the ''Five Civilized Tribes'' that had adapted to the white man's world. He proposed the sale of inexpensive lands to the poor and squatters rather than have it pass to land speculators and agents. These ideas were ahead of his time and brought his political undoing. His motto was ''Be sure you're right, then go ahead,'' but due to his division with Jackson and his cronies, Crockett lost his seat in Congress. He turned his attention westward to Texas, as Sam Houston had before him, and was killed at the battle of the Alamo.

The legendary ''king of the wild frontier'' who ''killed him a b'ar when he was only three'' was immortalized in the popular press, movies, television series, ballads and yarns.

Some of the fanciful escapades attributed to Crockett in **The Davy Crockett's Almanac** include: Davy climbs the lightning and greases it with a bottle of rattlesnake tallow; he sails up Niagara Falls on the back of an alligator; he climbs the peak of Daybreak Hill, greases the earth's axis with bear's fat, and snatches a piece of sunrise to take back down as fuel for cooking his bear steak. Furthermore, he picked his teeth with a pitchfork, combed his hair with a rake, fanned himself with a hurricane, could whip his weight in wildcats, drink the Mississippi dry or slide down the slippery end of a rainbow.

The 1840 **Crockett Almanac** included the following adventure:

Colonel Crockett and the Bear and the Swallows

People tell a great many silly stories about swallows, stated Crockett. Some say that if you kill one your cows will give bloody milk, or that they keep Christmas and New Year's among the little fishes at the bottom of some pond. But he claimed that they slept all winter in the hollow of an old sycamore and that he had learned this the hard way.

Out early one spring, ''...with my rifle on the banks of the Tennessee, making up my opinion about matters and things in general,'' he heard a noise like a clap of thunder. But it was a clear day without a cloud, and after hearing the clap again, he placed the sound with a big swarm of swallows as they flew out of the trunk of a hollow sycamore tree.

''Now I thought to myself that them ar little varmints were doing some mischief in the tree, and that it were my duty to see into it. For you see just then I felt hugeously grandiferous, for the neighbors had made me a justice of the peace.''

Since the bark of a sycamore is very smooth, he cut a sapling and leaned it against the larger tree and climbed it to the opening at the top. As he peered down into the darkness of the hollow, the younger tree broke beneath him, and, losing his balance, he fell all the way to the bottom of the tree, landing up to his knees in droppings from the birds, and found himself ''the nastiest critter ever you saw..., and how to get out I didn't know; for the hole was deep, and when I looked up I could see the stars out of the top.

''Presently I put my hand into some thing as soft as a feather bed, and I heard a awful growling, so that I thought it was the last trump sounding to fall in and dress to the right for the day of judgment. But it was only an old b'ar I woke out of his winter nap, and I got out 'Butcher' [his knife] to see which were the best man. But the critter was clean amazed and seemed to like my room better than my company and made a bolt to get out of the scrape, most cowardly.

''Hollo, stranger!'' said Davy. ''We don't part company

Maple and poplar leaves collect in a pool along the Phillips Hollow Trail in the Cherokee National Forest in Tennessee.

without having a fair shake for a fight.'' First he grabbed hair on the bear's posterior, but it began to come out in his hands. ''I got hold of his stump of a tail with my teeth, and then I had him fast enough. But still he kept on climbing up the holler, and I begun to sorter like the idea; for you know he couldn't get up without pulling me up after him.... I quickened his pace with an awful fundamental poke with my Butcher, jest by way of a gentle hint. Before long we got to the top of the tree, and then I got to the ground quicker than he did, seeing he come down tail foremost. I got my shooting iron to be ready for him.

''But he kinder seemed to got enough to my company, and went off squealing as if something ailed his hinter parts, which I thought a kind of curious; for I've no opinion of a fellow that will take a kick, much less such usage as I give him. However, I let him go; for it would be unmanly to be unthankful for the service he done me, and for all I know he's alive yet....''

Big Bald Mountain, on the route of the Appalachian Trail, on the Tennessee/North Carolina line

Story of Andrew Jackson and Russell Bean

The deeds of Andrew Jackson, heroic and otherwise, eventually led him to the Presidency of the United States. In addition to his military prowess at the Battle of New Orleans, he had a reputation as a great Indian fighter. In 1812 Jackson's army of volunteers, along with a large contingent of Cherokee warriors, destroyed a rebellious Creek Nation at the battle of Horseshoe Bend. This was probably the largest single Indian battle ever fought within the bounds of the United States. More than 1,000 Creeks were killed in the fight. Some accounts of the battle have claimed that the Cherokees saved the day for Jackson by a surprise attack across the river at the Creek rear, and even saved Jackson himself. It was an irony lamented by Cherokee chief Junaluska after Jackson betrayed the tribe.

More than any other individual, Jackson bears responsibility for the shameful ''Trail of Tears'', in which the Cherokee were rounded up like cattle and marched to the Indian lands of the West. One third of the tribe died as a result of the trip.

As a young lawyer and judge, Jackson practiced for a time at Jonesborough, the first capital of Tennessee.

"Judge Jackson was holding court at a shanty in the frontier village of Jonesborough, Tennessee, and dispensing justice in large and small doses, as seemed to him required in the case before him. One day during court, a great hulking fellow, a rifle maker named Russell Bean, armed with pistol and scalping knife, took it upon himself to parade before the shanty courthouse, and cursed the judge, jury, and all there assembled, in set terms.

" 'Sheriff,' sang out the judge, 'arrest that man for contempt of court, and confine him.'

"Out went the sheriff, but he soon returned with the word to the judge that he had found it impossible to take the offender.

" 'Summon a posse, then,' said the Judge, 'and bring him before me.'

"The sheriff went out again, but the task was too difficult; he could not, or dared not, lay his hands on the man, nor did any of the posse like the job any better than he did, as the fellow threatened to shoot the first skunk that came within ten feet of him.

"At this the judge waxed wroth, to have his authority put at defiance before all the good people of that vicinity; so he cried out, 'Mr. Sheriff, since you cannot obey my orders, summon me; yes, sir, summon me.'

" 'Well, judge, if you say so, though I don't like to do it; but if you will try, why I suppose I must summon you.'

" 'Very well,' said Jackson, rising and walking toward the door, 'I adjourn this court ten minutes.'

"The ruffian was standing a short distance from the shanty, in the center of a crowd of people, blaspheming at a terrible rate, and flourishing his weapons, and vowing death and destruction to all who should attempt to molest him.

Fall colors along the slopes of Mount Mitchell, North Carolina

The western North Carolina Blue Ridge, viewed from Craggy Gardens in the Pisgah National Forest

"Judge Jackson walked very calmly into the center of the group, with pistols in hand, and confronted him.

"'Now,' said he looking him straight in the eye, 'surrender, you infernal villain, this very instant, or I'll blow you through!'

"The man eyed the speaker for a moment, without speaking, and then put up his weapons, with the words, 'There, judge, it's no use, I give in,': and suffered himself to be led by the sheriff without opposition. He was completely cowed.

"A few days after the occurrence, when the man was asked why he knocked under to one person, when he had before refused to allow himself to be taken by a whole company, he replied:

"'Why,' said he, 'when he came up, I looked him in the eye, and I saw shoot, and there wasn't shoot in nary other eye in the crowd; and so I says to myself, says I, hoss, it's about time to sing small, and so I did.'"

—James Parton,
Life of Andrew Jackson, 1888

Moonrise at dusk, viewed from Mount Mitchell, North Carolina

How the Moon Got its Spots

When the Sun was a young woman she lived in the East, while her brother, the Moon, lived in the West. The girl had a lover who used to come every month in the dark of the moon to court her. He would only come at night, and always left before daylight, and although she talked with him she could not see his face in the dark. He would not tell her his name, so she was wondering all the time who it could be. In her curiosity she devised a plan to learn his identity.

The next time he came to visit, they were sitting together in the dark, and she began to caress his face, saying, "Your face is so cold: you must have suffered from the wind," and pretended to be concerned for him. But unknown to him, she had slyly rubbed charcoal from the fireplace onto her hands, and the next night when the Moon came up in the sky, his face was covered with spots where she had rubbed it. He was so much ashamed to have her know that he had been her suitor that he kept as far away as he could at the other end of the sky all night.

Ever since he tries to keep a long way behind the Sun, and when he does sometimes have to come near her in the west, he makes himself as thin as a ribbon so that he can hardly be seen.

—*Retold from James Mooney,*
Myths of the Cherokee*, 1900*

In this story the sun is female and the moon male, but it was more common for these roles to be reversed. In Seneca fiction the Moon is an old woman who can be seen sewing.

Linville Gorge was named for an unfortunate William Linville. In 1766 he and his son were killed and scalped while exploring the area. This view overlooks the rims of the Linville Gorge Wilderness Area, 1,500 feet above the ravine and river. This is on the Brown Mountain side of the canyon, where strange lights have been reported since frontier days. The lights have sparked scientific studies as well as supernatural explanations.

The Mysterious Brown Mountain Lights

Long ago, before the American Revolution, a hunting party from the coastal colonies was camped below the crest of the Blue Ridge Mountains in the area now known as Brown Mountain. Fascinated by the scenery, wildflowers and animals of the highlands, one of the gentlemen hunters wandered away from the party and was lost in the trackless wilderness. After a long, fruitless search, the hunter was given up for dead, and his companions returned to their plantations in the lowlands. But one of his trusted servants, unwilling to give up his beloved master for lost, returned to the mountain to continue the search and was never heard from again. Warm summer nights his lantern can still be seen wandering along the ridges, testament to loyalty and duty that has crossed the centuries.

This story and other local folklore attempt to explain the mysterious Brown Mountain Lights of western North Carolina. Another of the tales has the wandering spirit on the mountain belonging to the ghost of an Indian princess, searching with a pine knot torch for her lost lover. Skeptics have labeled the eerie glow that seems to move around the ridges as mirages created by distant trains, planes or automobile headlights, refracted through the humid atmosphere, or natural occurrences of static or luminous gases.

Another account of the mysterious lights along the ridge recalls the restless soul of a pioneer woman who was murdered and buried in a shallow grave somewhere in the area. Her spirit keeps moving so that her relatives will never be able to see her badly disfigured face and body. Her lantern may be spotted as she moves from place to place among the hills.

Origin of the Pleiades and the Pine Tree

Long ago, when the world was new, there were seven boys who used to spend all their time down by the townhouse playing chunkey. (This was a popular game among many woodland tribes and involved bowling a stone game wheel along the ground and sliding a curved stick after it to strike it.) The boys wouldn't help their mothers in the fields or do other chores, no matter how much their mothers scolded.

One day when the boys returned home hungry, their mothers had boiled a pot of game wheels instead of corn; dipped the stones out and said, ''Since you like chunkey better than the cornfield, take the stones now for your dinner.''

The boys were very angry, and went down to the townhouse, saying, ''As our mothers treat us this way, let us go where we shall never trouble them any more.'' They began a dance and went round and round, praying to the spirits to help them. Finally, the mothers became worried and went looking for them only to see them gradually rising from the earth as they circled. The mothers tried to reach their sons to bring them back, but it was too late. One of the women managed to reach her boy with one of the game poles and pulled him back, but he came down so hard that he was buried in the earth.

The boys circled higher and higher until they went

A view southwest from the rims of Linville Gorge, North Carolina

up to the sky, where we see them now as the cluster of stars called Pleiades. The people grieved long after the departed youths, and the mother whose boy had gone into the ground came every morning and evening to weep over the spot where he had disappeared, until the ground became damp with her tears. At last a little green shoot arose from the spot and grew until it became the tree we now call the pine. So it is believed that the pine tree is of the same nature as the stars and holds in itself the same bright light.

Pine knots were used as torches and to turn back the darkness of council fires in the village townhouses from that time until now.

—*Retold from James Mooney,*
Myths of the Cherokee*, 1900*

Many myths resemble fairy tales and were told as entertainment, as well as for symbolism and moral instruction. Another story which takes place in the Black Mountain range is the story of how the Terrapin beat the Rabbit.

Looking along the summits of the mountains from the top of Mount Mitchell, it is easy to imagine the Terrapin crossing the ridges of Mount Craig, Celo Knob and other nearby ridges:

A Race Between the Terrapin and the Rabbit

The Rabbit was renowned among all the animals as a great runner. The Terrapin on the other hand, although a brave warrior and very boastful, was considered to be slow. But since the two were always debating their speed they decided to settle the matter with a race. A day was set, and the course was to be across four of the high peaks of the Black Mountains. The Rabbit was so sure of himself that he spotted the Terrapin the first one.

The Terrapin gathered his friends the night before the race and told them that he knew he couldn't beat the Rabbit, but he wanted to stop the Rabbit's boasting. So they devised a plan.

The next day all the animals gathered to watch the race, the Rabbit was with them at the starting line, and the Terrapin had gone ahead to the top of the first ridge as agreed. When the starting signal was given the Terrapin was seen to cross the first ridge top, and the Rabbit bounded up the mountain, expecting to win the race before the Terrapin could get down the slope. But as he got to the top, he saw the Terrapin disappearing over the hill ahead. Increasing his speed, he jumped up the next ridge, only to catch a glimpse of the Terrapin again crossing the mountain ahead of him. In disbelief, the Rabbit jumped for all he was worth to overtake the Terrapin, only to see him cross the fourth ridge to win the race. The Rabbit collapsed in exhaustion, not even finishing the course.

So how could the plodding Terrapin beat the Rabbit? It seems that all his friends looked just like him, and before the race began, one of his clan hid in the tall grass atop each ridge. When they saw the Rabbit coming they crossed the crest, then disappeared back into the underbrush. With the Terrapin waiting near the last ridge he was easily declared the winner.

Because the Rabbit lay down and lost the race, later competitors in ball play or other contests would prepare a soup of rabbit hamstrings to pour over the path of their opponents, so that they might become tired in the same way as the boastful Rabbit and lose the game.

—*Retold from James Mooney*
Myths of the Cherokee, *1900*

The high crest of the Black Mountains, including Mount Mitchell, is seen in the background of a meadow of catawba rhododendron in western North Carolina.

The Origins of Corn and Game

The origins of corn and game are common themes in the stories of American Indian tribes, as in the Cherokee tale of Kanati (The Lucky Hunter) and his wife Selu (Corn):

Long years ago, soon after the world was made, a hunter and his wife lived with their two sons at Pilot Knob in the Black Mountains. One was the adopted magician "Wild Boy" who led his brother in original mischief. At that time their lives were without effort, Kanati always returned from his hunts with a fat buck or doe, or perhaps a couple of turkeys, and Selu always had a plentiful supply of corn and beans. But one day the boys set out to discover their father's secrets, first following him to discover how bows and arrows were made, then to a secret place where all the animals were kept, inside a cave on the north side of Mount Mitchell.

They watched as Kanati rolled aside a stone from the opening and killed a buck as it ran out. Later the boys returned to the cave to try their hand at bringing back game. They raised the rock and a deer came running out, but as they took aim to shoot, another, and another raced out, and in their confusion all the deer escaped into the forest along with droves of rabbits, raccoons, and all the four legged animals. Then came great flocks of turkeys and all the birds. Their flight darkened the sky and their beating wings made a sound like thunder. Hearing the noise, Kanati rushed to the place where he kept the game, but he was too late. He found the two boys standing by the rock, but all the birds and animals had fled, and since that time people have had to seek them all over the world.

In his anger Kanati went into the cave and kicked the covers off four jars in the corner and swarms of bedbugs, fleas, lice and gnats began to bite and sting the boys, and these pests survive to this day.

Returning home tired and hungry the boys asked their mother for something to eat. "There is no meat," Selu replied, "but wait here awhile and I will get you something." But the mischievous boys followed her to her storehouse and watched her through a hole in the chinking as she rubbed her stomach and her basket was magically filled with grain. Seeing this they agreed that their mother must be a witch and decided to kill her. Of course, she knew their thoughts and instructed them that they should prepare the ground and drag her body over it, so they would always have corn. And from her blood and body, all the bounty of the fields were born.

The adventurous boys eventually became the Little Men, or Thunder Boys, that lived in the west and taught the early people to plant seed for grain and the songs to bring the game from the forest. When they talk to each other we hear low rolling thunder in the west.

—Retold from James Mooney
Myths of the Cherokee, *1900*
and Charles Lanman,
Letters from the Allegheny Mountains, *1849*

View from the Blue Ridge Pinnacle, reached by a one-and-one-half-mile walk from the Blue Ridge Parkway in North Carolina

Snakeroot has conflicting roles in folklore. Reputed to turn the milk of cows that eat the plant poisonous, it was also thought to be useful in a number of folk and Indian remedies, including antidotes for snakebite, cough and toothache.

Snakeroot carpets the summit of Mount Mitchell beneath a ghost forest of Fraser Fir trees. Mount Craig and Celo Knob in North Carolina are in the background.

Trillium blooms on the high slopes of Mount Mitchell, North Carolina. The plant was used in eye treatments among several Native American tribes, and in Cherokee lore it was believed to be a love potion if the roots were ground and added to food.

Surrounded on each side with a deep wall of woods, I enjoyed the serenity of the evening in silent meditation; every thing which I saw and heard taught me a lesson which required not the powers of oratory to embellish it.

—Francis Baily,
**Journal of a Tour in the Unsettled Parts of the
United States of North America in 1796 and 1797**

A view westward across the grassy balds from Tennent Mountain in the Shining Rock Wilderness Area along the Art Loeb Trail

Here we halted some time in order to admire the beauties of the place.... The scenery of the craggy mountains, covered with trees to their very top, contrasted with the smooth level of the plain, afforded us a view highly picturesque, novel, and enchanting; and one which we could not but dwell on with pleasure.

—Francis Baily,
**Journal of a Tour in the Unsettled Parts of the
United States of North America in 1796 and 1797**

Mountain ash trees lean away from prevailing west wind on Balsam Knob in the Shining Rock Wilderness Area of North Carolina.

Two friends that have met on a mountain may always claim that as their level, and their souls may always sail out over hills that are hard to climb, over valleys that are tilled with sweat and reaped with Trouble's sickle, over cities whose commerce perplexes religion, over societies whose laws and forms oppress a free spirit; from such a height we may look down and understand...
—Sidney Lanier, **Tiger·Lilies,** 1864

Story of the Slant Eyed Giant

A long time ago the highland balds and streams around the Shining Rock Wilderness area were the domain of a great, slant eyed giant named Tsulkalu. He was reputed to be the owner of all the game in the mountains, and his favor could be very beneficial to the Indian settlements along the river valleys and foothills. In one of these old villages, named Kanuga, at the forks of the Pigeon River (near today's Waynesville, North Carolina), there lived a widow with a daughter who wished to marry.

The mother cautioned the girl that she should only marry a good hunter so that they would have someone to take care of them and provide meat. When a stranger began courting the girl she told him of her mother's wishes, and he replied modestly that he was a great hunter. He only came to visit at night, but after that he always brought a deer or other gifts for the mother.

Eventually the mother insisted on meeting her daughter's suitor, and, after much persuasion, he agreed to stay one morning. The mother was shocked to see that her daughter's lover was a great giant, with long slanting eyes, and she ran crying from his sight. Tsulkalu was terribly hurt and angry and returned to his own country in the high mountains. After their child was born, the girl also left the village to join her husband. Although they sometimes visited the area of the girl's village, and left enough food to feed all its people, from that time they lived in the high country and had many children.

Her brother, while exploring the balds looking for her, was drawn to their home inside the great halls within the mountains by the sound of drums and dancing. Hoping to restore the giant's favor with the village, since game had become scarce, the brother asked how they could get Tsulkalu to return. He told his brother-in-law that if the villagers would stay inside their townhouse and fast for seven days he would come to visit them and bring gifts, but that no one must raise the war whoop when he came.

After seven days of fasting those gathered in the townhouse heard a great roar coming from the mountains and, although they were all frightened, none made a sound. But unfortu-nately, as the noise grew closer, like great boulders tumbling down the hillsides, a visitor from another village ran from the group and gave a war cry. Believing that his orders were not obeyed, the giant turned back to the mountains with diminishing thunder, taking his gifts with him and vowing that they would never see him again.

Perhaps the giant and his family still scamper and dance along the remote highland balds. Tracks along the stony

Depressions in the stony summit of Balsam Knob in the Shining Rock Wilderness Area of North Carolina

Streaks in the rock strata atop the crests of the Shining Rock Wilderness Area are supposed to be tracks left by the giant Tsulkalu as he dragged game along the highlands.

ridge crests of the Shining Rock are said to be where the giant dragged his game, and others look like great footprints. According to local folklore, the giant tribe's old dancing grounds were below the Devils Courthouse, near today's Blue Ridge Parkway, and the round dome of Looking Glass Rock covered their home within the mountains.

—*Retold from James Mooney,*
Myths of the Cherokee*, 1900*

A rainbow hangs over Ivestor Gap in the Shining Rock Wilderness Area of western North Carolina.

"The great Thunder and his sons, the two Thunder boys, live far in the west above the sky vault. The lightning and the rainbow are their beautiful dress. The priests pray to the Thunder and call him the Red Man, because that is the brightest color of his dress. There are other Thunders that live under waterfalls and travel on invisible bridges from one high peak to another where they have their townhouses. The great Thunders above the sky are kind and helpful when we pray to them, but these others are always plotting mischief. One must not point at the rainbow, or one's finger will swell at the lower joint."

—James Mooney,
Myths of the Cherokee, 1900

The sun breaks through the clouds in a view from the Shining Rock Wilderness Area of the North Carolina highlands.

Color symbolism played an important role in the shamanistic systems of all the Indian tribes. Among the Cherokee, each of the cardinal points has its corresponding color and meaning and guardian of that region. The Red Man lives in the east and is the spirit of power, triumph, and success; black represents death and dwells in the west; blue symbolizes the north and defeat or trouble; and white, for the south, stands for peace or happiness.

Milky quartz boulders atop Cold Mountain in the Shining Rock Wilderness Area

*All animated nature, in whatever degree, is in their eyes
a great whole from which they have not yet ventured to
separate themselves.*

—James Mooney,
Myths of the Cherokee, 1900

Bluets bloom in the Shining Rock Wilderness Area.

James Mooney

James Mooney was a dedicated scholar and researcher of Cherokee history, religion, ceremonies, songs and language. His collection of their myths, legends and sacred formulas was the first major documentation of their lore. Much of his material was gathered with the help of tribal elders who remembered and practiced their old ways and was written or dictated by the shaman of the tribe. Recorded in their communities from 1887 to 1890, the material was published as a series of reports of the American Bureau of Ethnology to the Secretary of the Smithsonian Institution, in Washington, DC as **Myths of the Cherokee and Sacred Formulas of the Cherokee**.

A summer rainstorm passes through the Cowee Mountains near Cherokee, North Carolina.

Here…terminates the great Vale of Cowee, exhibiting one of the most charming natural mountainous landscapes perhaps anywhere to be seen; ridges of hills rising grand and sublimely one above and beyond another, some boldly and majestically advancing into the verdant plane, their feet bathed with silver flood of the Tanase, whilst others far distant, veiled in blue mist, sublimely mounting aloft, with yet greater majesty lift up their pompous crest, and overlook vast regions.

—William Bartram, 1775,
The Travels of William Bartram

William Bartram

William Bartram became famous as a botanist in the late 1700s. He was the first of his discipline to travel into the interior of the southern Appalachian region. He traveled inland to the head waters of the Little Tennessee River cataloging and classifying many of the area's plants. The journal of his trip into the highlands in 1775 conveys a sense of awe the wayfarer experienced before the pristine world that greeted him.

A hiker trail across Wayah Bald and Winesprings Bald

Late summer wildflowers atop Wayah Bald, near the William Bartram and Appalachian Trails junction

(near the route he probably took through the mountains), in the Nantahala National Forest, commemorates his journey.

Wayah Bald and the gap below it were favorite spots for ambush as enemies of the Cherokee traveled along the aboriginal path that crossed the mountains in this area. Translated as ''Wolf'' in the Cherokee language, the history of the Wayah area is told in fierce images of courage and stealth. A British army en route to relieve the garrison at Fort Loudon was defeated here in 1760 by Cherokee warriors, thus causing the fall of the remote outpost (the only British-manned fort to fall to American Indians). The following year a similar attack on a larger expedition failed and opened the heartland of the tribe to total destruction by the invaders. But the Wayah area has also seen the passing of Shawnee and Seneca raiders and was probably the route across the mountains taken by Hernando DeSoto in 1540.

Three Contests Between the Rabbit and the Deer

In the beginning the Deer had no horns, even the bucks' heads were completely smooth. The Deer was a great runner, and the Rabbit was a fine jumper, and the animals were all curious to know which could go farther in the same time. They talked about it a good deal, and at last arranged a match between the two and made a nice large pair of antlers for a prize to the winner. They were to start together from one side of a thicket and go through it, then turn and come back, and the one who came out first was to get the horns.

On the fixed day all the animals were there, with the antlers put down on the ground at the edge of the thicket to mark the starting point. While everybody was admiring the horns the Rabbit said: "I don't know this part of the country; I want to take a look through the bushes where I am to run." They thought that seemed fair, so the Rabbit went into the thicket. Even then the Rabbit was known as one of the greatest tricksters, and when he was gone so long the other animals suspected that he must be up to one of his pranks. They sent a messenger to look for him, and away in the middle of the thicket he found the Rabbit gnawing down the bushes and pulling them away until he had a road cleared nearly to the other side.

The messenger turned around quietly and came back to tell the other animals. When the Rabbit came out at last they accused him of cheating, but he denied it until they went into the thicket and found the cleared road. They agreed that such a trickster had no right to enter the race at all, so they gave the horns to the Deer, who was admitted to be the best runner, and he has worn them ever since. They told the Rabbit that as he was so fond of cutting down bushes, he might do that for a living thereafter, and so he does to this day.

This should have settled the rivalry between them, but it didn't. The Rabbit felt sore because the Deer had won the horns and resolved to get even. One day soon after the race he stretched a large grapevine across the trail and gnawed it nearly in two in the middle. Then he waited on the Deer to come along.

Soon the Deer wandered down the path and asked what he was doing. The Rabbit responded in his usual boastful manner that he was fine, and furthermore, "I'm so strong that I can bite through that grapevine at one jump."

The Deer could hardly believe this and wanted to see it done. So the Rabbit ran back, made a tremendous spring, and bit through the vine where he had gnawed it before. The Deer said, "Well, I can do it if you can." So the Rabbit stretched a larger grapevine across the trail, but without gnawing it in the middle. The Deer ran back as he had seen the Rabbit do, made a spring, and struck the grapevine right in the center, but it only flipped him back and threw him over on his head. He tried again and again, until he was all bruised and bleeding.

"Let me see your teeth," at last said the Rabbit. So the Deer showed him his teeth, which were long like a wolf's teeth, but not very sharp.

"No wonder you can't do it," said the Rabbit; "your teeth are too blunt to bite anything. Let me sharpen them for you like mine. My teeth are so sharp that I can cut through a stick just like a knife." And he showed him a black locust twig which he had shaved off as well as a knife could do. The Deer thought that was just the thing. So the Rabbit got a hard stone with rough edges and filed and filed away at the Deer's teeth until they were worn down almost to the gums.

"It hurts," finally said the Deer; but the Rabbit

assured him that it always hurt a little when they began to get sharp; so the Deer kept quiet.

"Now try it," at last said the Rabbit. So the Deer tried again, but this time he could not bite at all.

"Now you've paid for your horns," said the Rabbit, as he jumped away through the bushes. Ever since then the Deer's teeth are so blunt that he can not chew anything but grass and leaves.

The Deer was very angry at the Rabbit for filing his teeth and determined to be revenged, but he kept still and pretended to be friendly until the Rabbit was off his guard. Then one day, as they were going along together talking, he challenged the Rabbit to jump against him. Now the Rabbit was a great jumper, as every one knows, so he agreed at once. There was a small stream beside the path and the Deer said:

"Let's see if you can jump across this branch. We'll go back a piece, and then when I say Now! then we'll both run and jump."

"All right," said the Rabbit. So they went back to get a good start, and when the Deer gave the word Now! they ran for the stream, and the Rabbit made one jump and landed on the other side. But the Deer had stopped on the bank, and when the Rabbit looked back the Deer had conjured the stream so that it had grown to be a large river. The Rabbit was never able to get back again and is still on the other side. The rabbit that we know is only a little thing that came afterwards.

—Retold from James Mooney,
Myths of the Cherokee, 1900
(Myths 26, 27 and 28)

A fawn walks along the Appalachian Trail between Clingmans Dome and Silers Bald in the Great Smoky Mountains National Park.

The Sacrifice of Tsali

"To prevent escape the soldiers had been ordered to approach and surround each house, so far as possible, so as to come upon the occupants without warning. One old patriarch, when thus surprised, calmly called his children and grandchildren around him, and, kneeling down, bid them pray with him…while the astonished soldiers looked on in silence. Then rising he led the way into exile. A woman, on finding the house surrounded, went to the door and called up the chickens to be fed for the last time, after which, taking her infant on her back and her two other children by the hand, she followed her husband with the soldiers."

In 1838 the United States army under General Winfield Scott entered the lands of the Cherokee nation with orders to start every Indian on the path west before another moon had passed. Their lands had been guaranteed by sovereign treaties for as long as the grasses grow and the rivers flow, and there had been peace within the region for many years. But the soldiers quickly executed their orders and began to move the helpless people into stockades to prepare for the trip west.

As Indian families were marched from their homes and fields, marauding bands of scavengers carried away their livestock and other possessions and dug up graves looking for anything of value. Pushed along by gun or bayonet point, most of the disposed farmers and herders went peacefully to the concentration camps. But all were not so submissive.

One old man named Tsali, or "Charley", was seized with his wife and brother and all their families. On the trek from their homes, they were treated brutally and Tsali's wife was prodded with a bayonet to urge her to travel faster. Speaking in their own language, Tsali urged his relatives to join him in a desperate bid for liberty. At his signal they turned on their captors and attempted to wrest the weapons from the hands of the soldiers. The attack was so sudden and unexpected that in the struggle one of the troops was killed, and the others fled back to their stockade.

The families dashed for the remote reaches of the mountains and lived for a time in a cave at the head of Deep Creek in the Smoky Mountains. Other groups made their way into hiding in the fastness of the Nantahalas, Snowbirds, Cheoahs, and Unicois and lived on nuts, berries, herbs and small game. Hoping to avoid the work and danger of hunting them all down, Scott sent word that if they would surrender Tsali, then he would allow the remainder to stay behind in the hills until their appeals to stay in the east could be resolved.

Told of the proposal, Tsali, his two sons, and brother walked to the junction of the Tuckasegee and Little Tennessee River the next morning to be executed. The younger son was spared due to his youth, but the others stood over their freshly dug graves. Members of their own tribe were ordered to do the killing. Facing their executioners without blindfolds, the men of Tsali's family bravely sacrificed themselves for the rest of their kinsmen.

—From Mooney, Lanman and others

Fire pink and yarrow in bloom

I fought through the Civil War and have seen men shot to pieces and slaughtered by the thousands, but the Cherokee removal was the cruelest work I ever knew.

—Z.A. Zile, Georgia Volunteers,
later Colonel in Confederate Army

Late summer asters bloom beside the headwaters of Deep Creek in the Great Smoky Mountains National Park.

The Cowhide Treaty

"…The Indians were believed to have come out of the earth, and therefore they own it and are to go back into it. The white people, on the other hand, were created later out of the foam of the sea. They first begged to put one foot on shore to rest themselves a little, and the Indians consented, but afterward the newcomers complained that it was tiresome to stand on but one foot and they asked to be allowed to set the other ashore. This also was granted. Next, the whites wanted to buy from the Indians as much land as could be covered with a hide, and when the Indians agreed they cut the hide into strips and made it surround a large area…"

—*John R. Swanton,*
Native Creek History Legends*, 1928*

Legend of a Great Water Monster

Along this stretch of the Little Tennessee River there once lived a monstrous water creature. Perhaps not as fearsome as its relatives living in the Neus River in the North Carolina Tuscarora country, which could devour entire canoes filled with warriors, but it was a huge snake-like monster and was a constant threat to children who wandered alone near the shore.

Also living along high cliffs in the bend of the stream, near its junction with Citico Creek, a great hawk, larger than any that live today, had its den in a cave and also terrorized the villages. Sometimes it would carry off dogs or children in its great talons.

Finally one of the great medicine men devised a plan to rid the area of both monsters. One day, while the bird was away hunting, the medicine man climbed down the cliff from above. Finding the nest unattended, he threw all the great hawk's young into the stream far below. The water monster raised its head out of the water to feast on the unexpected bounty. But the big serpent was spotted by the returning mother hawk as it ate the last of the chicks. In her anger she plucked the water monster from the river and carried him high into the air, tearing it to pieces and throwing them down as she flew. It is said that great holes in the rocks along the valley still show the marks of the falling pieces.

—Retold from James Mooney
***Myths of the Cherokee**, 1900*

Tales of great water serpents and giant fish were common among all the tribes around the perimeters of Appalachia. Another of the water monsters from Cherokee lore was the great Dakwa.

The Hunter in the Dakwa

The Dakwa was a gigantic fish that lived in the Little Tennessee River at its junction with Toco Creek. One day it wrecked a dug out canoe of hunters as they crossed the stream, tossing them all into the air and swallowing one of the men in one gulp as he came down. It was extremely hot and dark in the belly of the monster fish and the warrior knew he would quickly suffocate if he didn't take quick action. Feeling around inside the beast's stomach, his hand felt a large mussel shell, and using this as a knife he began to hack at the dark insides of the fish. Hot blood poured over him until it seemed as if he would drown if he didn't smother first. But he continued to lash out, slashing with the sharp edged shell, until he began to see daylight. He finally was able to cut his way free and kill the monster which had terrorized his people along that stretch of the stream.

—Retold from James Mooney,
***Myths of the Cherokee**, 1900*

Redbuds and native dogwood bloom beside the Little Tennessee River below Fontana, North Carolina.

Mountain craftsmen prized the wood of the Dogwood for its hard, tight grain and used it as mauls, axes and in numerous other tools and crafts. The wild and cultivated varieties of the tree are prolific and grow over a wide range. Recent evidence lists the tree among those sensitive to rising acidity in the rains and subsequent accumulation in the soils of the region. Although still prolific, dogwood is also declining rapidly in many areas due to a blight.

The dogwood tree appears in anonymous folklore of the region related to Christian tradition:

Long ago the Dogwood was one of the tallest and straightest trees that grew, but to its shame it was used to fashion the cross of Jesus when he was crucified. Since that time the Dogwood has been in mourning. Dwarfed and gnarled, its limbs and trunk grow crooked and it never reaches a great height. The tree's bloom—four petals pierced at the ends and its ringed crown in the middle—is symbolic of Christ on the cross. The Dogwood blooms in mountain altitudes near Easter.

There is a belief in many Native American religions that every event that occurs at a place will always live at that spot. Rock cairns were erected where a loved one had died or an important event occurred, and each wayfarer would add a stone or pebble in respect for the souls that had passed before. Ancient spirits might be pleased or unhappy depending on whether their deaths were properly atoned for or the memories of their lives respected as they watch from the spirit realm. According to these old beliefs, the spirits of our ancestors loved these mist-laden valleys and upright hills and gave their being to them. These ideas recall an Appalachia that is a sacred ground, revered, and anointed by the blood and lives of our grandfathers. Standing in the solitude of these now silent shores, amid the deep purple and grey of dusk, today's wanderer might feel a sudden, unexplainable chill. Watching hypnotic reflections of fireflies and a hazy yellow sliver of new moon, it is easy to imagine laughter and ancient campfires in the narrow lonely coves, quiet hopeful eyes watching and curious whispers floating among the looming hemlock, pine and oak. Along the region's woodland paths there is a gentle aura of ancient spirits that have passed before, and the enfolding highlands beckon with serenity for those yet to come seeking their peace and strength.

Following the American Revolution, the Cherokee people living in the numerous villages along the Little Tennessee River had determined to live in peace with the white man, but hostilities continued to the south and west as settlers poured into the region. In 1788 a campaign of retaliation for attacks by Indians along the frontier was mounted by an army of volunteers under John Sevier (who later became Tennessee's first governor), and they entered the Little Tennessee and Hiwassee valleys looking for hostile warriors. Village chiefs who counseled for peace, including Tassel and Abram, gathered at the home of Abram at the town of Chilhowie, at the junction of Abrams Creek and the Little Tennessee River, under a white flag of truce. In Sevier's absence a relative of a slain settler entered Abram's cabin and brutally murdered all of the Indian peace delegates. The site now lies beneath the waters of Chilhowie Lake.

In the generation following the American Revolution white settlers took the best lands along the Tennessee and Little Tennessee Valleys. One of the more notable of the emigrants to the Little Tennessee Valley was the young Samuel Houston.

Sam Houston spent his adolescence along the valley and spent more of his time with the Cherokee than he did on his mother's farm. Named "The Raven" by his adopted Cherokee family, Houston went on to fight in the company of Andrew Jackson and David Crockett in the defeat of the Creeks at Horseshoe Bend in Alabama. He became a colorful and popular figure on the frontier. As a congressman and then Governor of Tennessee, he was a strong advocate of Indian rights. When he moved west to Texas he served as its first governor.

Another native of the winding valleys of the Little Tennessee and Hiwassee Rivers was the inventor of the Cherokee syllabary, Sequoyah. His ranks as one of the great individual accomplishments of history. Although illiterate, he had heard of the white man's "Talking leaves" in which they could record and transmit their thoughts. He devised an alphabet of 86 characters, with each symbol representing a sound, for the Cherokee language. His system skipped the necessity of learning to spell words; once the alphabet was learned, the person could read and write. A majority of the Cherokee people mastered the system within months, a degree of literacy much higher than that of their white neighbors. The tallest trees on earth, the Sequoyah Redwoods, a national park, and a nuclear power plant honor his memory.

Living in the isolation of Appalachia after the frontier moved on to the plains and mountains of the west, many subsistence farmers adopted the same fierce attachment and reverence for the land as the Indian had before him. In this land of make do or do without, mountain families developed a culture of self sufficiency that in many cases included hunting and gathering combined with agriculture. These mountaineers were close observers of the natural world, and the generations passed in harmony with the soil and seasons. But in the face of rediscovery by an insatiable industrial economy, with its rush to exploit mineral rights, cheap labor and space for resort developments, fatalistic Christian stoicism and graves of ancestors in small family plots served them no better than

Coneflowers and ironweed line the banks of Chilhowie Lake. The winding valley of the Little Tennessee River was the home of the Lower Cherokee villages. Most of the sites are now beneath the lake.

the ideals practiced by the Indians. The results have been near wastelands left by the extractive industries and chronic disregard for even weak environmental standards for air and water quality by a host of chemical, oil, paper and other industries. Driven by poverty in a land of plenty, the native mountaineer had been herded off the highlands to factory reservations and trailer parks, frequently becoming fodder for the dangers of underground mines, low-paying drone assembly lines, and service sector posi-

tions catering to those behind their ''No trespassing'' notices.

Insulated from the earth in the mobile societies of our cities and suburbs, the natural world has lost its awe and sacred status. Earth bound philosophies, where life is dependent on forces greater than oneself, have been replaced by the religions of conspicuous consumption, immediate gratification and ''Every man for himself''.

The Origin of Disease and Medicine

All the members of the animal kingdom were angry with people and wanted to declare war on them for their carelessness and abuse. They complained in council that humankind had little respect for his fellow creatures, spread too quickly over the world, and killed and ate the animals. It was agreed that they should seek revenge for this carnage.

First, the bears met in their townhouse under Mount Kuwahi (now Clingmans Dome), located in Great Smoky Mountains on the border of Swain County, North Carolina, and Sevier County, Tennessee, to plan an attack on people.

They intended using bows and arrows as people did, but found that their claws became caught in the strings and the idea was given up. Unable to agree on how to wage their war, they disbanded to roam the forest and thickets, but will still imitate men when they stand and fight when cornered.

The other animals were more successful in their plans. They agreed to unleash all sorts of disease to attack people, and except for the intervention of the plants, may well have killed them all. The plants were friendly to people, and to help them, they made every tree, shrub and weed the antidote for part of the mischief released by the animals. The knowledge of which plants to use and the sacred formulas for driving away the malevolent spirits has been passed down the generations by shaman and priests of the Cherokee.

—Based on James Mooney,
Myths of the Cherokee

Numerous wild plants were used by aboriginal medicine men in their conjuring and sacred formulas to drive away evil influences and break spells invoked by offended animal spirits, witches or other diabolic forces. The plants were used as teas, tonics, poultices, blown on the patient, or as incense in elaborate ceremonies. They also had an important role as charms and preventatives to ward off malevolence, to cleanse, or to purify. All of life was attended to with great ritual to maintain a harmonious balance with the world around them, or to atone to offended spirits. Each day began with required bathing at dawn, even if ice on streams had to be broken first. There was no concept of a natural death or sickness. In this system there was little sickness before contact with whites, and many lived to great ages.

Much of this plant lore was added to traditional remedies in the practice of folk medicine on the Appalachian frontier far from doctors and hospitals. Many of the herbs and plant derivatives have been found to be beneficial, with high vitamin or mineral content, or good sources of unrefined drugs (such as willow bark and roots for headaches and other ailments). Other treatments such as poultices, teas and tonics, or brews made from ferns to treat rheumatism and arthritis, or the benefits of ginseng, are viewed with skepticism, or as placebos.

Flame azalea and pine trees line the banks of Fontana Lake, an impoundment of the Little Tennessee River. This area probably witnessed the passing of William Bartram, Sidney Lanier, Sam Houston, Sequoyah, the Cherokee and unknown tribes before them.

The evening still and calm, all silent and peaceable, a vivifying gentle breeze continually wafted from the fragrant strawberry fields, and aromatic calycanthean groves on the surrounding heights, the wary moor fowl thundering in the distant echoing hills, how the groves and hills ring with the shrill perpetual voice of the whip-poor-will!
—William Bartram,
The Travels of William Bartram, 1775

The Enchanted Lake

Westward from the headwaters of the Oconaluftee river, in the wildest depths of the Great Smoky Mountains is the enchanted lake of Atagahi. Although all the Cherokee know that it is there, no one has ever seen it, for the way is so difficult that only the animals know how to reach it. Should a stray hunter come near the place he would know of it by the whirring sound of the thousands of wild ducks flying about the lake, but on reaching the spot he would find only a dry flat, without bird or animal or blade of grass, unless he had first sharpened his spiritual vision by prayer and fasting and an all-night vigil.

Because it is not seen, some people think the lake has dried up long ago, but this is not true. To one who had kept watch and fasted though the night it would appear at daybreak as a wide-extending but shallow sheet of purple water, fed by springs spouting from the high cliffs around. In the water are all kinds of fish and reptiles, and swimming upon the surface or flying overhead are great flocks of ducks and pigeons, while all about the shores are bear tracks crossing in every direction. It is the medicine lake of the birds and animals, and whenever a bear is wounded by the hunters, he makes his way through the woods to this lake and plunges into the water, and when he comes out upon the other side, his wounds are healed. For this reason the animals keep the lake invisible to the hunter.

—Retold from James Mooney,
Myths of the Cherokee.

The enchanted lake was said to be below the crest of the ancient Kuwahi, today's Clingmans Dome.

Sidney Lanier

In the years just preceding the Civil War the family of author and poet Sidney Lanier owned a resort in the Little Tennessee River Valley. As a teenager he roamed up and down the valley and over many of the high ridges of the Smokies.

The sun sets behind the Great Smoky Mountains in a view from Clingmans Dome.

The hills sit here like old dethroned kings, met for consultation: They would be very garrulous, surely, but the exquisite peace of the pastoral scene below them has stilled their life; they have forgotten the ancient anarchy which brought them forth; they dream and dream away, without discussion or endeavor.

—Sidney Lanier,
Tiger Lilies, 1864

Dusk along the Appalachian Trail between Clingmans Dome and Silers Bald

The foreground of such a landscape in summer is warm, soft, dreamy, caressing, habitable; beyond it are gentle and luring solitudes; the remote ranges are inexpressibly lonesome, isolated and mysterious; but everywhere the green forest mantle bespeaks a vital present...
—Horace Kephart,
Our Southern Highlanders, 1913

Hemlock and mixed Appalachian hardwoods along the Chimney Tops Trail in the Great Smoky Mountains National Park

Fall colors at Grotto Falls in the Smoky Mountains of Tennessee

Mid-summer blooming great rhododendron line a branch of the Little Pigeon River on the Alum Cave Bluffs Trail in the Great Smoky Mountains National Park.

This wilderness blossoms as the rose; and these desolate places are as the garden of God.
—Timothy Flint, 1833

Flint Visits the Rabbit

In the old days, before the Master of Things had decided how everything should be, Flint lived up in the mountains. All the animals hated him because he had helped to kill so many of their friends and relatives. They used to get together to talk over means to put him out of the way, but everybody was afraid to venture near his house until the Rabbit, who was then the boldest leader among them, offered to go after Flint and try to kill him. They told him where to find him, and the Rabbit set out and at last came to Flint's house.

Flint was standing at his door when the Rabbit came up and said, sneeringly, "Hello! Are you the fellow they call Flint?" asked the Rabbit. "Yes; that's what they call me," answered Flint. "Is this where you live?" Rabbit inquired. "Yes, this is where I live." All the time the Rabbit was looking about the place trying to study out some plan to take Flint off his guard. He had expected that Flint might get lonesome up in the mountains by himself all the time and maybe invite him into the house, so he waited around a little while and made more small talk. But when Flint made no move, he said, "Well, my name is Rabbit; I've heard a good deal about you, so I came to invite you to come see me."

Flint wanted to know where the Rabbit's house was, and he told him it was down in the broom-grass field near the river. So Flint promised to make him a visit in a few days. "Why not come now and have supper with me?" said the Rabbit, and after a little coaxing Flint agreed and the two started down the mountain together.

When they came near the Rabbit's hole the Rabbit said, "There is my house, but in summer I generally stay outside here where it is cooler." So he made a fire, and they had their supper on the grass. When it was over, Flint stretched out to rest, and the Rabbit got some heavy sticks and his knife and cut out a mallet and wedge. Flint looked up and asked what that was for. "Oh," said the Rabbit, "I like to be doing something, and they may come in handy." So Flint lay down again, and pretty soon he was sound asleep. The Rabbit spoke to him once or twice to make sure, but there was no answer. Then he came over to Flint, and with one good blow of the mallet, he drove the sharp stake into his body and ran with all his might for his own hole; but before he reached it there was a loud explosion, and pieces of flint flew all about. That is why we find flint in so many places now. One piece struck the Rabbit from behind and cut him just as he dived into his hole. He sat listening until everything seemed quiet again. Then he put his head out to look around, but just at that moment another piece fell and struck him on the lip and split it, as we still see it.

—Based on James Mooney,
Myths of the Cherokee

The rocky spine of mountains on the Appalachian Trail on the southwest slope of Clingmans Dome

Witch Hobble, with fall colors, thrives amid ferns and fallen fraser firs on Clingmans Dome. The evergreen firs are dying on all the high peaks of the Appalachians due to combined factors of acid rain deposition, severe weather, and infestations of balsam wooly aphids.

Old hunters in the Smoky Mountains region say that bears, when chased on a hunt, would frequently lead the dogs through thickets of the smaller variety hobble bush, Dog Hobble. The density and sharp edges of the brush would cause the dogs to falter, and the bear would bound right through it. Apparently from the name, Witch Hobble was even stronger medicine that could restrain or cause a witch to stumble. This large shrub is one of the first to bloom in the spring and is one of the first to display its fall colors ranging from lemon yellow to deep scarlet and ruby.

Mountain maple in fall colors stands beside a branch of the Little Pigeon River along the Chimney Tops Trail in the Great Smoky Mountains National Park.

How harmonious and sweetly murmur the purling rills and fleeting brooks, roving along the shadowy vales, passing through dark, subterranean caverns, or dashing over steep rocky precipices, their cold, humid banks condensing the volatile vapours, which fall and coalesce in crystalline drops, on leaves and elastic twigs of the aromatic shrubs and incarnate flowers.

—William Bartram,
The Travels of William Bartram, 1775

Origins of the Night Sky

"Iroquois tradition tells us that the sun and moon existed before the creation of the earth, but the stars had all been mortals or favored animals and birds.

"Seven little Indian boys were once accustomed to bring at eve their corn and beans to a little mound, upon the top of which, after their feast, the sweetest of their singers would sit and sing for his mates who danced around the mound. On one occasion...their heads and hearts grew lighter as they flew around the mound, until suddenly the whole company whirled off into the air.... Higher and higher they arose, whirling around their singer, until, transformed into bright stars, they took their places in the firmament, where, as the Pleiades, they are dancing still, the brightness of the singer having been dimmed, however, on account of this desire to return to earth.

"A Party of hunters were once in pursuit of a bear when they were attacked by a monster stone giant, and all but three destroyed. The three together, with the bear, were carried by invisible spirits up into the sky, where the bear can still be seen, pursued by the first hunter with his bow, the second with the kettle, and the third, who, farther behind, is gathering sticks. Only in fall do the arrows of the hunters pierce the bear, when his dripping blood tinges the autumn foliage....

"An old man, despised and rejected by his people, took his bundle and staff and went up into a high mountain where he began singing the death chant. Those below who were watching him saw him slowly rise into the air, this chant ever growing fainter and fainter, until it finally ceased as he took his place in the heavens, where his stooping figure, staff, and bundle have ever since been visible, and are pointed out as the old man.

"An old woman, gifted with the power of divination, was unhappy because she could not also foretell when the world would come to an end. For this she was transported to the moon, where to this day she is clearly to be seen weaving a forehead-strap. Once a month she stirs the boiling kettle of hominy before her, during which occupation the cat, ever by her side, unravels her net, and so she must continue until the end of time, for never until then will her work be finished.

"As the pole star was ever the Indian's guide, so the northern lights were ever to him the indication of coming events. Were they white, frosty weather would follow; if yellow, disease and pestilence; while red predicted war and bloodshed; and a mottled sky in the springtime was ever the harbinger of a good corn season."

—Erminnie A. Smith, **Myths of the Iroquois**, *1880. Second Annual Report of the Bureau of Ethnology to the Secretary of the Smithsonian Institution, 1880-1881 Washington, DC, 1883, Pages 80-81. (For a slightly different version of the Pleiades origin see page 48.)*

An autumn quarter moon rises behind fraser firs on Clingmans Dome.

How People Came into the World and the Origins of Clans

"When the Creek Indians came to know anything of themselves, it was to find that they had been for a long series of generations completely buried and covered as it were in a dense fog impenetrable to their powers of vision. Being unable to see, they were dependent on their other senses, especially that of touch, in their efforts to obtain subsistence.

"In their quest for food, the people very naturally became separated, straying away from each other in groups, and each group was aware of the existence and locality of its neighbors only by calling to them through the obscuring fog, each adopting the precaution not to stray out of calling distance of some other of the scattered groups.

"After a great while there arose a wind from the east that gradually drove the fog from the land. The group of people who first saw clearly the land and the various objects of nature now rendered visible by the dissipating fog were given the name of the Wind clan. It is related that, among the many things they were now able to see, the first animate objects observed by the people of the Wind clan were a skunk and a rabbit which appeared to have accompanied them during their existence in the obscuring fog. While the people did not adopt either of these as their patronymic, they did declare them their nearest and dearest friends. So well is this understood by the full blood Creek Indian, that it is universally understood to be the duty of the sons of the Wind clansmen always to extend to these animals protection and defense from physical injury or ridicule, saying 'They are my fathers.'

"As the fog continued to recede and disappear before the driving east wind, other groups of people came to light; and, as each looked about, it adopted as the patronymic of the clan by which it would thereafter be known, the first live animal which had emerged from the fog along with it.

"In this manner three other clans—The Beaver, the Bear, and the Bird—were established, who, together with the Wind, have always been known as Hut-hak-ul-kee-d (the whites) and recognized as leaders in the establishment and maintenance of peace in the nation. The Wolf clan is kindred to the Bear clan, but without the political prestige of the latter. All the other clans, which are very numerous, were formed in the same manner and are known as Tsi-loak-hok-ul-kee (speakers of a different language) as distinguished from the Hut-hak-ul-kee, or Whites."

—John R. Swanton, *Creek Social Organizations and Usages*, *42nd Annual Report of the Bureau of American Ethnology to the Smithsonian Institution, 1924-25, Washington, DC, 1928, pages 112-113.*

John Muir

John Muir was one of America's most revered naturalists. Founder of the Sierra Club, he is credited with originating sentiment for preserving a part of our natural world during the early decades of this century. His was an important voice crying for wilderness preservation during an era known for the exploitation of both people and lands by the barons of industry.

An emigrant from Scotland, Muir spent his early years in the midwest but began his life's work of exploring and advocacy of the natural earthscape with a trek through the foothills of the Cumberland and Blue Ridge mountains between St. Louis, Missouri, and Savannah, Georgia, then across Florida. During his ''Thousand-mile Walk to the Gulf,'' he passed through the Cumberland Gap and down parts of Cumberland River. The John Muir Trails, in the Big South Fork National Recreation Area of Tennessee and Kentucky as well as a path beside the Hiwassee River in southeast Tennessee, commemorate that walk.

A sweetgum tree in fall color stands in early morning fog beside the Hiwassee River.

How the Earth Was Created

"The time was in the beginning, when the earth was overflowed with water. There was no earth, no beast of the earth, no human beings. They held a council to know which would be best, to have some land or to have all water. When the council had met, some said, 'Let us have land, so that we can get food,' because they would starve to death. But others said, 'let us have all water,' because they wanted it that way.

"So they appointed Eagle as chief. He was told to decide one way or the other. Then he decided. He decided for land. So they looked around for someone they could send out to get land. The first one to propose himself was Dove, who thought that he could do it.

Accordingly they sent him. He was given four days in which to perform his task. Now, when Dove came back on the fourth day, he said that he could find no land. They concluded to try another plan. Then they obtained the services of Crawfish. He went down through the water into the ground beneath, and he too was gone four days. On the fourth morning he rose and appeared on the surface of the waters. In his claws they say that he held some dirt. He had at last secured the land. Then they took the earth from his claws and made a ball of it. When this was completed they handed it over to the chief, Eagle, who took it and went out from their presence with it. When he came back to the council, he told them that there was land, an island. So all the beasts went in the direction pointed out and found that there was land there as Eagle had said. But what they found was very small. They lived there until the water receded from this earth. Then the land all joined into one."

—John R. Swanton, **Creek Religion and Medicine**, *1928. 42nd Annual Report of the Bureau of American Ethnology to the Smithsonian Institution, 1924-25, Washington, DC, 1928, Pages 487-488; citing Speck Memoirs American Anth. Asso., vol. II, pt. 2, pp.145-146.*

Autumn in the Joyce Kilmer/Slickrock Wilderness Area of North Carolina

Standing Indian Area

Prior to 1838 many of the high crest of the Nantahalas were believed to harbor the homes of the Immortals/Spirit People. One day a delegation of the Immortals told the villagers of the Little Tennessee River Valley and others surrounding the mountain passes that a great danger was approaching and, if they wished, all the people could come to live with them. Many decided to take their offer. Those planning to accompany the Immortals were told to gather in their townhouses to fast and pray, but that when they came for them no one was to make a sound.

When the Immortals came on the appointed day, they picked up the townhouses to carry them through the air to their dwelling places on the high balds. But as one townhouse began to rise, some of those inside became frightened and screamed. This startled the Spirit People briefly and they dropped a corner of the building, and this became the mound at the present site of Franklin, North Carolina, but the others were transported safely to the homes of the immortals where they live today. Many of the rock formations in the mountains are said to be the remains of the old longhouses, but that the people have gone far away.

Another rock formation, resembling the body of a man, once stood on the remote summit of one of the Nantahala chain. Now called Standing Indian Mountain, it is on the route of the Appalachian Trail. But the stone man was struck by lightning and scattered around the peak many years ago. How he came to be frozen on the peak is uncertain, but it was probably because he failed in his sentry duties long ago. He was finally allowed to rest, but only after most of his people had departed to the land of gathering shadows.

The summit of Standing Indian Mountain along the Appalachian Trail in North Carolina

The river and falls around the Tallulah Gorge of north Georgia were believed to be the haunt of powerful Thunder Spirits who had their home in a cave behind the falls. To the Indians of the region, it was a place of danger to be avoided. One Cherokee brave who was enchanted by one of the sisters of Thunder married her and went with her through the secret passages to their home. But after finding their world too scary, he returned to his old village, only to sicken and die on telling of his adventure.

Today the old rumbling magic of the gorge has been tamed to flow through the lines of Georgia Power and electrify a modern world.

The Creation of Man

God at first created the sun and the moon. One day while walking about on the earth, becoming lonely, he said, "I will make a human being to keep me company." He held his way until he came to an uprooted hemlock, which had raised a great pile of earth with its upturned roots. Now, the roots of the hemlock are very numerous and slender and are covered with tufted rootlets for, as the tree grows on thin, pale sandy soil, it needs many feeders to provide the necessary sustenance. God made a human being from the earth piled up among the roots of this tree. There were so many small fibers in this earth that the human being was seemingly hairy, and the soil was so poor and light-colored that he had a pale, sickly complexion. God breathed on him, and he stood up and walked. Then God looked at him from behind the roots of the tree, but being not pleased with his creation, he resolved that he would try again.

Tallulah Gorge in north Georgia

Maple leaves and pine needles line the stream banks in the Raven Cliffs Wilderness Area of north Georgia.

God soon came to a walnut tree lying uprooted, which had pulled up with its roots a mound of black earth. From this earth God made another human being. As he looked at him, he saw that, being black, he had too much color. So God was not satisfied with this piece of work, either.

Going on farther, he came at last to an uprooted sugar maple. There the earth had a fine deep color; so out of this God made the third human being, whose body was smooth and firm and of a full rich tint. And God, pleased with his looks, said, "He will do; he looks like me." This last human being was an Indian; thus the Indian was the native human being.

—Folk tale collected by Jeremiah Curtin and J.N.B.Hewitt, **Seneca Fiction, Legends, and Myths,** *pages 168-169. 32nd Annual Report of the Bureau of American Ethnology to the Secretary of the Smithsonian Institution, 1910-1911. Washington, DC, 1918.*

Blood Mountain/Slaughter Gap Area

The intensity and brutality of intertribal wars in the ancient Appalachia is nearly incomprehensible. Among virtually all the eastern woodland nations, war was their ''Beloved Occupation''. All young males were expected to go on the warpath, and until they had killed or performed some heroic act, they were treated with contempt. In many tribes until they attained the rank of warrior, with the addition of some form of the title ''Man-killer'' to their name, they were abused and forced to perform humiliating services for those who had proven themselves. The pressure was so great to ''Bring back hair'' that unsuccessful war parties were known on occasion to murder members of their own tribe to obtain scalps. Kidnaping and unmerciful torturing to death of prisoners, this by the women of the tribe, was common practice.

However, the show of bravery in the face of danger was more important than the annihilation of their enemies, and most exchanges were in the form of small raids. Until the introduction of firearms, the number of fatalities in battles was usually small. But due to their laws of blood for blood, the fighting was nearly perpetual.

Blood Mountain, Slaughter Mountain, and the gap between them, Slaughter Gap, in north Georgia, apparently was the scene of a particularly ruthless battle between the Creek and Cherokee. The tribes had been mortal enemies for many years, and the Cherokees kept sentries at strategic points to warn of danger. One day it was discovered that a large band of Creek was headed into the Cherokee country, and all the warriors rallied to intercept the intruders. An ambush was laid along the route of the Creek, and so many were killed that it was said that the streams running from the mountains were colored red. These places were named to remember the carnage that took place there.

Blood Mountain was also known as one of the homes of the Immortals, the spirit people. They were believed to have a home under the mountain, evidenced by the rock formations on its crest resembling ancient townhouses and smoke that came from its springs in winter. These spirit people could be called on to help the Cherokee when they were in danger.

Mountain laurel begin to bloom on Blood Mountain in Georgia.

Trees bud atop the rocky summit of Blood Mountain, along the Appalachian Trail, in north Georgia.

A small waterfall and autumn leaves in the Raven Cliffs Wilderness Area of north Georgia

This world, as a glorious apartment of the boundless palace of the sovereign creator, is furnished with an infinite variety of animated scenes, inexpressibly beautiful and pleasing, equally free to the inspection and enjoyment of all His creatures.

—William Bartram,
The Travels of William Bartram, 1775